THE
SILENT
INTELLIGENCE

THE INTERNET OF THINGS

DANIEL KELLMEREIT | DANIEL OBODOVSKI

DnD Ventures
San Francisco, California

For information and requests, please contact: info@thesilentintelligence.com

For media contacts: media@thesilentintelligence.com

Web: www.thesilentintelligence.com

Facebook: https://www.facebook.com/thesilentintelligence

LinkedIn: http://www.linkedin.com/groups/Silent-Intelligence-Internet-Things-5036434

Twitter: @SilentIntelBook

YouTube: http://youtu.be/2-LvsxJ-ls0

ISBNs:
978-0-9899737-0-0 (Soft Cover)
978-0-9899737-1-7 (eBooks)

CONTENTS

FOREWORD

When Daniel Obodovski asked me to write the foreword to *The Silent Intelligence,* my first thought was, "You mean the part of the book that most people skip over? I can do that." My second thought, once I realized he was serious, was, "Um, sure." So here we are.

I was lucky enough to start participating in the Internet of Things movement in 1999, although at the time we were not at all sure how to even refer to the potential market. While I had always expected adoption to happen sooner, I am still very optimistic that everything will be connected. It's just a matter of time. In the early 2000s, we thought the benefits for companies to connect their products were so obvious that there would be a revolution and that it would be over in a few years.

Why would any company delay in making a relatively small investment in a technology that enhances their brand, lowers their costs, provides better customer service, differentiates their product offerings, builds recurring relationships with customers, provides higher customer satisfaction and more? In fact you could even turn on your coffee machine at work remotely! It was so obvious to us that we thought people would just do it, and within three to five years the whole world would be connected. In fact, sometimes we worried we might be too late to the dance.

In retrospect, like most adoptions of a disruptive technology, it didn't happen in two years. Or even five. Adoption of M2M has been distributed across many markets, and fourteen or fifteen years later, it feels like it has snuck up on us.

Why has it taken so long for the world to catch on to what some of us have known for over a decade? It is because in the majority of cases, new technologies that can disrupt business models take much more time to be accepted than anyone in that market wants or expects. In the U.S. market, it took cell phones about twenty years to get to major mass-market penetration. Cloud computing (think Software as a Service, timesharing) can trace its origins back many, many years. With a handful of exceptions, tablets being possibly the best-known outlier, technology adoption takes years.

I think we were fooled, like many early market entrants, into thinking we would move right from the visionary customers and early adopters directly into mainstream adoption. The reality, well explained in Geoffrey Moore's book *Crossing the Chasm*, is that in order to get across that chasm between the early adopters and the early majority, you need to package that technology into something that is easy for companies to consume. This means not only offering a complete solution, but offering it from brands that are trusted and companies that provide global scale.

One method I use to get a sense of where we are in market maturity is what is happening to the early entrants in an ecosystem. Are they burning through venture capital, announcing the same customers over and over, going out of business, merging with other small players, or getting acquired by big players interested in the space? A significant indicator for M2M was that once the wireless carriers got involved in mergers and acquisitions, that the tipping point into mass adoption was occurring.

This is exactly what I experienced. First Qualcomm acquired my M2M platform company, nPhase, in 2006. This was a huge validation for the market space and a call for others to start looking more seriously at the sector. Then, a couple of years later, we spun it out as a joint venture between Qualcomm and Verizon Wireless and eventually sold it to Verizon Wireless.

What is the significance of wireless carriers entering a space by M&A? From my perspective, it is that their channels touch almost every company in the world. When they focus on an initiative, they have the ability to raise the water level and dramatically increase the market size. And that is exactly what they are doing.

The funny thing is that when the mass adoption does come, it seems like no big deal. Over time we become acclimated to new technology. In fact, it is almost when the technology doesn't seem so gee-whiz anymore that mass-market adoption has occurred. It becomes an invisible, silent, part of our everyday experience.

Well, that feels to me like where we are with M2M and the Internet of Things. I am not sure if you can even buy a car today that does not come standard with connectivity, or at least have it available as an option. You expect that your e-reader or tablet is going to seamlessly connect to the cloud somewhere and download your book or newspaper. You expect that you can track the progress of your FedEx package or even the pizza delivery driver. You expect your printer to tell you that you are out of ink, you expect to track plane flights online, and that when you have a problem with your (computer, air compressor, construction equipment, MRI machine, truck, whatever) that someone can remotely connect in and at least diagnose a problem, if not actually fix it. That is the promise of a connected world. And it is here, albeit quite a bit later than I thought it would be.

This is why I think this is a perfect time for publication of The Silent Intelligence. The Internet of Everything is still not that well understood in the general business community, and this book brings organization to a complex market. It includes interviews with many of those who have taken an active part in developing the market. It provides multiple, valuable perspectives of the Internet of Things. You will learn about some of the obvious and not-so-obvious impacts this technology is having on our everyday lives and how you can apply these concepts going forward. You will read about some of the ways companies are leveraging these capabilities to enhance their businesses. And on the way, you will enjoy an entertaining, informing, and informed read by two authors whom I greatly respect.

Steve Pazol

April, 2013

INTRODUCTION

On a cold day in November 2011, the two of us were sitting in the conference room of Detecon USA, on the top floor of a high-rise overlooking the stunning San Francisco Bay, discussing technology trends. We used to discuss things like cloud services, big data, mobile health care, and so on. We had these discussions every couple of months, and it seemed like the view of the San Francisco Bay encouraged big thoughts and interesting ideas. We often talked about the Internet of Things, or Machine-to-Machine (M2M) connectivity, which is a more technical term for it. The topic appeared confusing on one hand and exciting on the other, because it was incorporating many other technology trends.

It's hard to know which one of us first came up with the idea to write a book about M2M, but we both loved the idea immediately and decided to embark on this project. Indeed, Benjamin Disraeli once said, "The best way to become acquainted with a subject is to write a book about it." Little did we know what we were getting ourselves into . . .

Like a lot of people in the industry, we were intrigued by the emerging growth of Machine-to-Machine communication. Our respective skill sets and backgrounds are complementary— Daniel Kellmereit is the CEO of a top consulting company; he's written several books and has a well-structured, analytical mind. Daniel Obodovski has led multiple M2M projects at Qualcomm and has practitioner's experience. Both of us have an extensive network of contacts in the technology/information systems industry, and specifically in the M2M space.

We decided to reach out to our respective networks and interview those with the most experience to hear and convey their stories. In the process, we also met and interviewed other amazing people in the space: pioneers, thinkers, and visionaries.

One of the things we discovered was how much of the Internet of Things was actually already happening around us, without us really noticing, because the subject is very diverse and not covered by the popular media nearly as much as, for example, social networks or smartphones. That gave us the idea to call our book *The Silent Intelligence*, because we feel like machines and things around us are becoming more intelligent and are doing so silently.

Although the demands of our respective jobs, combined with the inherent complications of co-writing a book, were challenging, we both felt it was necessary to write *The Silent Intelligence*—for ourselves and for you, our readers. With determination and commitment, we overcame the challenges this collaborative project presented, to deliver, over a year later, the finished book you hold in your hands.

The main subject of this book is how connecting the physical world around us to the virtual world of the Internet can result in huge gains. By the *physical world* we mean things like cars, buildings, industrial machinery, home appliances, medical devices, bicycles, plants, animals, and human bodies.

By *gains* we mean, for example, recovering lost or stolen items using embedded GPS tracking devices, remotely monitoring a patient's health using tiny body sensors and thus preventing a heart attack, or monitoring the temperature and security of your home—from anywhere in the world.

The potential is enormous, but so are the challenges. As Kelly Venturini of M2M Certified put it, "Everybody wants to get connected and they don't freaking know how to do it."

Much has been written about the Internet of Things in publications such as the *Economist*, *Financial Times*, the *New York Times*, *McKinsey Quarterly*, and *Harvard Business Review*, as well as multiple research studies and white papers by Harbor Research, ABI, and Frost & Sullivan, to name a few. We wanted to build upon these sources, but also go further and deeper in our examination, to answer these fundamental questions: What is the Internet of Things? How is it coming about? What are the key trends? What is the potential? What needs to be done to succeed in this space?

Our goal was to first make sense of this vast topic for ourselves, by analyzing the mentioned sources, considering our own experience, and talking to the industry thought-leaders and subject-matter experts. Then we wanted to share what we were discovering with our readers. Our hope is that this book will help you better understand this space, realize the potential, and recognize the challenges and complexity. Finally, we want to share our views on how to overcome obstacles and identify the most promising areas for investment and job creation.

The first four chapters of the book take a thirty-thousand-foot-high view of the subject, while the last three chapters go into more practical detail and examine the specific challenges, opportunities, and examples.

In chapter 1, we start by defining the subject and what impact it might have on our everyday lives. Here we also talk about the nature of the terms *Machine-to-Machine* and the *Internet of Things* and others, such as *embedded computing* and *smart services*. Then we examine the history of the topic. We followed the advice of Peggy Smedley of *Connected World*, who suggested we look back before we look forward. It was important for us to understand where the Internet of Things came from, which trends preceded it, and, more importantly, which trends are aligning now to facilitate the exponential growth of new services, businesses, and opportunities in this space.

Chapter 2 talks about the technology ecosystem of M2M and its various players. In this chapter, we attempted to logically split the ecosystem into three main areas: data collection, data transport, and data analysis. Here we also talk about the main technical challenges of the space and the opportunities that present themselves in addressing these challenges.

Chapter 3 looks into the future of M2M and the Internet of Things and focuses on what this brave new world may look like. We ask some provocative questions: What role will humans play when a lot of decision-making is done by machines, and might humans ever become a bottleneck to realizing the Internet of Things vision? We also take a peek at what the ubiquitous connectivity between various devices may look like in real terms.

Chapter 4 is dedicated to the core industries of M2M. We picked connected cities, connected homes, connected health care, and connected cars. While these areas do not cover all the aspects of M2M (not even close), they do offer great examples of the impact Machine-to-Machine technology will have. We also hope this overview will help readers discover new areas for M2M and the Internet of Things on their own.

Chapter 5 starts by discussing the importance of well-defined use cases for the success of a technology or a business. We examine specific use cases in the M2M space that have been implemented with varying degrees of success. Comparing these provides a better map for what has been working and not working in M2M. We spend some extra time discussing the use case for body-worn fitness devices, using BodyMedia as an example.

Chapter 6 explores the topic of getting an M2M product to market and the surrounding challenges. Most of this chapter is based on specific firsthand experiences in launching M2M products and the lessons learned. The central part of this chapter is Mark Wells' story about how he built his company, Procon, from zero to one of the largest and the most successful companies in M2M.

Finally, in chapter 7 we analyze the investment attractiveness and opportunities of the M2M space, based on expert views and our own conclusions. This chapter answers the question: Where would and should you invest in M2M if you were an entrepreneur, individual, institutional investor, or a corporation willing to get involved in the M2M space?

In the process of writing this book, we interviewed many industry experts and thought leaders: Steve Pazol of nPhase and Qualcomm, Bill Davidson of Qualcomm, Glenn Lurie of AT&T, Glen Allmendinger of Harbor Research, Mark Wells of Procon, Steve Hudson of Omnilink, Kevin Ashton of Belkin, Dr. Sanjay Sarma of MIT, Assaf Biderman of MIT's SENSEable City Lab, Astro Teller of BodyMedia and Google, Bill Toone of ECOLIFE Foundation, Christian Busch of SAP, Ioannis Fikouras of Ericsson, Ivo Stivoric of BodyMedia, John Elliott of Accenture, John Major of MTSG, Peggy Smedley of *Connected World*, Ari Silkey of Best Buy and Zubie, Dermot O'Shea of Taoglas, Dr. Peter Kuhn of Scripps Research Institute, and Panos Nasiopoulos of the University of British Columbia. They tell fascinating stories about their experiences in the M2M space, which we did our best to capture and present in our book.

We hope the stories and conclusions in this book will help you better understand the space and its potential. And who knows? Perhaps you'll decide to start a new business, invest in the M2M vertical or industry, launch a new project, or just be as excited about this new growing world as we are. In any case, we wish you happy reading.

Daniel Kellmereit and Daniel Obodovski

San Francisco, June 2013

Chapter 1
HISTORY AND TRENDS

The future is already here—it's just not evenly distributed.
~ William Gibson

How can you tell if something will become so huge and powerful that it's going to change our lives and the way we do business? Below is a well-known story, popularized by Ray Kurzweil and retold as we know it, that illustrates the power of exponential growth.

> In ancient China a man came to the emperor and demonstrated to him his invention of the game of chess. The emperor was so impressed by the brilliance of the man's invention that he told the man to name his reward. The man asked for his reward in an amount of rice—that one grain be placed on the first square of the chessboard, two on the second,

four on the third, and so on—doubling the number of grains on each subsequent square.

Not being a very good mathematician, the emperor at first thought the reward to be too modest and directed his servants to fulfill the man's request. By the time the rice grains filled the first half of the chessboard, the man had more than four billion rice grains—or about the harvest of one rice field. At that point the man was rich. By the time the servants got to the sixty-fourth square, the man had more than eighteen quintillion rice grains (18×10^{18}), or more than all the wealth in the land. But his wealth and ability to outsmart the emperor came with a price—he ended up being decapitated.

In their recent book, *Race Against the Machine*,[1] Erik Brynjolfsson and Andrew McAfee, referenced the fable of the chess and rice grains to make the point that "exponential increases initially look a lot like linear, but they are not. As time goes by—as we move into the second half of the chessboard—exponential growth confounds our intuition and expectations."

As a result, in the early stages of a project or a new technology, it's very hard to discern whether or not something will experience exponential growth. As you will find in these next chapters, we believe this is exactly what is going to happen with the rise of the Internet of Things. If that's the case, the next decade and beyond is not only going to be more amazing from the standpoint of new devices and services coming to our

---

[1] Erik Brynjolfsson and Andrew McAfee, *Race Against the Machine: How the Digital Revolution Is Accelerating Innovation, Driving Productivity, and Irreversibly Transforming Employment and the Economy* (Lexington, MA: Digital Frontier Press, 2011), p.297.

everyday lives, but we will also see a dramatic change in our lives and the way we do business.

Many terms have been coined for the discussion of this topic: the *Internet of Things, Machine-to-Machine communication* or M2M, *ubiquitous computing, embedded computing, pervasive computing, smart services,* and, recently, General Electric added the term the *Industrial Internet* to the mix. One sign that we're dealing with something significant is that we are having difficulty naming it. According to Peggy Smedley, president of Specialty Publishing Co., editor-in-chief of *Connected World* magazine, and host of the "Peggy Smedley Show" podcast, "Every time we want to call it something new, people get confused and they wonder what the Internet of Things or M2M or embedded computing or the cloud actually mean. No single term fully describes the phenomenon. Everyone is seeing a part of the phenomenon that is closer to him or her and names it accordingly."

What is the phenomenon that we are struggling to name? Let's look at some examples.

Remote monitoring of industrial machinery through sensors helps avoid downtime. As Nokia mentions in their white paper, *Machine-to-Machine: Let Your Machines Talk,* "An ice-cream vending machine wants to tell the supplier that it's running out of chocolate cones, enabling the vending operator to better schedule his on-site visits."[2] Plants communicate if they need more water or food. Wearable electronics help people manage their weight or help pregnant women and their doctors monitor, in real time, the well-being of an unborn child. Mobile Personal Emergency Response Service (PERS) helps elderly or Alzheimer's patients automatically reach out to caregivers in an emergency.

---

[2] Nokia, *Machine-to-Machine: Let Your Machines Talk* (2004). http://www.m2m premier.com/uploadFiles/m2m-white-paper-v4.pdf.

Smart electric meters help consumers save on energy costs, while enabling the utility companies to optimize network load and avoid blackouts. Radio Frequency Identification (RFID) tags help us talk to the things around us, such as garments on the shelf of a store, to determine what's in stock and what needs to be reordered.

Connected cars help monitor performance, including tire wear. Cars communicate with one another to better navigate in traffic. Usage-based car insurance systems help insurance companies better manage risk, offer lower premiums to better drivers, and help drivers improve through instant feedback, thus making everyone safer.

Small tracking devices help recover lost children or pets. Covert tracking devices help law enforcement quickly recover stolen cargo. Smart cargo packages can ensure that valuable cargo arrives on time and undamaged.

And, if that's not enough, we can talk about tracking endangered animals, Tweeting plants, body sensors as small as temporary tattoos, connected contact lenses, driverless cars, and more.

All these things are possible because of M2M technology, and all these examples represent the Internet of Things. As Glenn Lurie, president of AT&T Emerging Devices Organization (EDO), says, "Any device that is connected is smart. Any device that is not connected is dumb. In the future, everything's going to be smart." Technology is making things around us smarter, yet we're often not even aware of it.

We called this book *The Silent Intelligence* because most of the activity and growth in the space has been happening outside of mainstream visibility. Who cares if, for example, their electric meter just became smart and connected? But the value and implications of this development on our lives is enormous. It's not about technology, but what it can do. As Astro Teller, director of new projects at Google, puts it, "What I care about is value being delivered to people. Usually it takes technology to do that, and I love technology in as much as it can help you deliver fantastic new value to people to solve problems or give them benefits they had never anticipated they could ever receive."

In a nutshell, the biggest benefit of the Internet of Things is that it gives us a unique opportunity to talk to the analog world around us (machines, people, animals, plants, things) in a digital way, with all the benefits of digital communication—speed of light, easy multiplication of data, and easy integration with other digital systems. All this, combined with wireless communication, produces an effect of *machine telepathy,* a condition where things can communicate over large distances unconstrained by wires.

Specifically, this gives us an opportunity to eliminate a lot of guesswork from everyday decisions. For example, by monitoring driving behavior, an insurance company collects a more accurate assessment of the risk profile than they would using just demographics, thus enabling them to fine-tune their rates. Another example is intelligent digital signs, which can recognize the area on a sign that people have been looking at most by tracking their eye movement. As Peggy Smedley says, "It's machines talking to machines giving us data, which is turned into information that we can act upon."

Assaf Biderman, associate director of MIT's SENSEable City Lab, puts it this way:

> Computers are becoming so small that they are vanishing into things. It's not Machine-to-Machine; it's thing-to-thing. The machine is irrelevant. That creates an ecosystem of things that talk to each other, and people are in the middle of it. If your environment is equipped with input-output nodes everywhere, it dramatically changes your relationship to your environment.

If we look back at the flow of technology development up until now, what might follow would start making a lot more sense. And it's true: The rapid growth of the Internet of Things and M2M flows logically from the overall computing and telecommunications technology development of the past several decades.

Astro Teller describes it like this:

> If you look at what happened with computers, they went through this relatively long period when they were big and clunky. People didn't see the need to have them in their homes until there were initial killer apps like spreadsheets and word processing. That helped to get the adoption started, but that's not why people have PCs anymore. Phones went through the same cycle. The killer app that caused the adoption was voice communication. Now that is not even the primary reason why people have smartphones—otherwise iPod Touches and iPads wouldn't be so popular. In both of those cases, we've seen an explosion of apps. Other things that you can do [with the installed base of these devices] turn out to be the reason, in the end, to dominate their value. Yet, we couldn't have made that argument at the beginning for either the PC or the phone. . . .
>
> I believe that wearable connected devices are going to go through the exact same process. The killer app today is weight management and fitness applications. But that's not why people are going to have body electronics—there will literally be tens of thousands of applications, some of which will be very conscious or explicit.

We will review examples of wearable connected devices in the following chapters.

Assaf Biderman makes a similar observation regarding the proliferation of networks:

> Thinking more completely about the early days of the Web: At the very beginning, once the concept was sort of worked out and tested, there was what we'd call an "installation era." Data warehouses were built and switches were put in place. These were mostly investments provided by either governments or by corporations with long-term visions. At the end, there was a critical mass of infrastructure. There was a skeleton that was strong enough to allow for bottom-up growth, and that bottom-up is really what created big value. Who knew, when the Web started, that the biggest rising thing a decade and something later would be Google? It came out of nowhere. I think that bottom-up movement so far provided the biggest value for the Web.

In the 1990s, the Internet became the standard for connecting personal computers and enterprise machines, which enabled a dramatic increase in productivity for individuals and corporations (specifically for order processing) and spurred electronic commerce. In the meantime, cellular networks were being built. Consumers' need for personal communications drove the rapid adoption of mobile phones, and with that, the innovation that was happening on mobiles—miniaturization, power efficiency, integration of sensors, antenna performance, and more. Finally, in the twenty-first century, personal computers and mobile phones merged, creating smartphones—one of the most successful platforms of all time. Now we are witnessing the next evolutionary step as mobility and computing are finding their way into smaller and more diverse devices—personal fitness, cars, home entertainment, health care, and so on.

The key trends that have been driving this technology development are:

- Miniaturization: Electronic devices have become smaller and more powerful, driven by Moore's Law,[3] but also by improvements in electric power management.
- Affordability: The costs of electronic components and networks have been consistently going down, also driven by Moore's Law to a large extent.
- De-wireization: More and more things are becoming wireless, which means they can be located anywhere. The growing ubiquity of cellular and Wi-Fi networks has driven this trend. The last wire to disappear will be the power cable, driven by advances in wireless power and power management.

Usually, once the necessary prerequisites are in place, the technology adoption that follows happens extremely fast. One good example is the rapid proliferation of smartphones. It took a long time to build 3G networks, ensure their stability, and create an ecosystem of applications, but once Apple introduced the first iPhone in 2007 and Android followed shortly after, smartphones took over the market within three years.

---

[3] The observation that the number of transistors on integrated circuits doubles approximately every two years. (Source: http://en.wikipedia.org/wiki/Moore%27s_law.)

We believe something very similar is about to happen in the M2M space. A big part of technology adoption is awareness. As Peggy Smedley says:

> It's all of these great minds that helped us understand what the technology can do for us, people like Robert Metcalfe or Steve Jobs and other great visionaries. They helped us really understand what the technologies can do, what the data behind the technologies can do. We have to look back before we can look forward.

We will talk more about the M2M technology ecosystem and its challenges in chapter 2; for now, let's look at the history of M2M or the Internet of Things.

"Something is happening. Things are starting to talk to other things. You will see it all around you. We know, because at Motorola, we're making it a reality."[4] What seems to be a timely statement was written over ten years ago in one of Motorola's advertisements. The vision was spot on, but ahead of its time. So when did M2M really start?

Steve Pazol, vice president and entrepreneur in residence (EIR) of Qualcomm, and founder and former CEO of nPhase, a pioneer of M2M, and a leading thinker in the space, says:

> If you think about telemetry, that's been going on since the man on the moon, right? If you think about sensors in different kinds of devices and assets, it's been done for a long time—thirty, forty years. You take a nuclear power plant, hopefully there are

---

[4] Motorola, *Aspira Intelligence Everywhere* (1999).

sensors and hopefully it's being monitored; maybe not wirelessly or maybe it's something proprietary.

In 1991, Mark Weiser, chief technologist at the Xerox Palo Alto Research Center (PARC), published an article on ubiquitous computing, which opens with these sentences: "The most profound technologies are those that disappear. They weave themselves into the fabric of everyday life until they are indistinguishable from it."[5] The article laid the foundation for many subsequent visions, resulting in the development of RFID, smartphones, and M2M solutions.

Glen Allmendinger, founder and president of Harbor Research, which arguably has done the most work analyzing the space, started working on the topic in the late '90s. He says:

> Don Davis [retired chairman of the board of Rockwell Automation, Inc.] commissioned us to take a look at essentially what we were then calling the *embedded Internet*. In August of 1998, I attended meetings that were about monitoring physical devices with wide-area networks and what kind of opportunities might be there. My joke when I got back to the office on Monday was that this subject's so complicated we won't have to think of another one before we die. . . .
>
> Then, roughly a year later, the then-CEO of Honeywell sponsored this huge project looking at asset management across half a dozen sectors of the economy, like health care, supply chain, and industrial. That's when all the ruminations pretty much took hold in

---

[5] Mark Weiser, "The Computer for the 21st Century," *Scientific American, Special Issue: Communications, Computers, and Networks,* September 1991.

my head and I realized that we were on to something very big.

At about the same time Kevin Ashton, general manager of Belkin and co-founder of the MIT Auto-ID Center, coined the term the *Internet of Things*. In the late '90s, Kevin worked at Procter & Gamble (P&G) as brand manager and was overwhelmed by the problem of tracking items throughout the supply chain. Kevin had a vision of the time when all objects in the supply chain would be able to connect to the Internet to report their whereabouts and status. According to that vision, information about objects—like Gillette razor blades or Pantene shampoos—would be stored on the Internet, and the smart tag on the object would just point to this information. In his presentation to the P&G board in 1998, Kevin called this vision the *Internet of Things*. To a large extent, this is exactly what ended up happening. Kevin's vision and the term, which he himself calls "ungrammatical," became extremely popular and spread like a meme.

With funding from P&G, Gillette, and a number of other global consumer products manufacturers, Kevin established the MIT Auto-ID Center together with Dr. Sanjay Sarma and a few others in April 1999. The purpose of the Auto-ID Center (currently MIT Auto-ID Labs) was to develop the Electronic Product Code—a global RFID-based identification system.

Sanjay Sarma describes the vision for Auto-ID:

> My colleague David Brock made the following inter-
> esting observation: Imagine you have Rosie the robot
> in your house and you say, "Get me a cup of coffee."
> It is supposed to go to the kitchen, find the coffee cup,
> pick it up, and bring it to you. David's observation was,
> "Why doesn't the robot just ask the damn thing [the
> cup] directly?" Everything is manmade. The coffee

cup is supposed to know how much it weighs or
what shape it is, what is the best way to approach it,
and so on. I just ask it instead of trying to recreate all
its information. I thought it was a beautiful insight.

Kevin Ashton continues:

Barcodes at the time were considered a quasi-auto-
matic data capture, but they are not automatic at all.
Barcodes are data-capture technology for humans,
while RFID is a capture technology for computers.
RFID is a way to hack the real world.

As things get wirelessly connected, Sanjay Sarma believes in
the proliferation of RFID. He thinks RFID readers will become
ubiquitous.

The economic downturn of 2001 only temporarily slowed
the unstoppable development of the Internet of Things. As a
matter of fact, things started picking up as early as 2002.

In 2004, Nokia published a white paper called *Machine to
Machine: Let Your Machines Talk*, which pointed out:

It is not only people who use telecommunication
and Internet technologies to communicate, but the
machines around us as well. This is called machine-
to-machine (M2M) communication. With tens of
billions of machines in the world, from home appliances to industrial machines, the potential is vast.

According to a legend, the term *M2M* was borrowed from
a then-popular Norwegian girl-pop duo of the same name that
was fancied by one of Nokia's executives. Around the same
time, in 2003, Peggy Smedley was getting *M2M Magazine* off the

ground. The magazine changed its name to *Connected World* in 2009. Peggy says the term M2M "has been a funny one, because people in the industry started calling all kinds of use cases and related technologies M2M."

Again, Glen Allmendinger:

> We never liked the term *Machine-to-Machine*. It did make fine sense if you were talking to technologists, but the minute you went off to talk to machine builders and people in the equipment world, it was much more of a techno-geek characterization of a much larger phenomenon.

At about the same time, Steve Pazol started nPhase, which had a significant impact on the growth of M2M, being first acquired by Qualcomm and later by Verizon. One of the first M2M applications nPhase pursued was monitoring the flashing lights on cell towers around airports. As Steve noted, "You didn't want airplanes running into cell towers; therefore, you had to monitor them. That drove the market."

In 2003, publishing a couple of pieces in the *Wall Street Journal* and the *New York Times*, Glen Allmendinger was approached by the *Harvard Business Review (HBR)*, which showed an interest in publishing an article on the subject but didn't want it called anything too technical. That's how, a year later, the term *smart services* was born. The article "Four Strategies for the Age of Smart Services" was published in *HBR* in 2005.[6]

The article generated a lot of interest in the topic, primarily from large industrial original equipment manufacturers (OEMs), who were trying to figure out how to connect their equipment.

---

[6] Glen Allmendinger and Ralph Lombreglia, "Four Strategies for the Age of Smart Services," *Harvard Business Review*, October 2005.

All they were really thinking about at the time was automating their service contracts. There was clearly a much bigger potential field out there than just remote services.

Then, in the second half of the 2000s, things started getting even more exciting. For the first time, a paradigm started shifting for wireless carriers. As the number of traditional mobile users was reaching saturation in developed countries, carriers started looking for other sources of revenue, and connecting machines to the network started making sense.

For a long time before that, carriers were obsessed with average revenue per user (ARPU) and were not interested in low-revenue-generating connections. But then in the summer of 2007, we had an interesting meeting with KDDI, a Japanese wireless carrier company. While American and European carriers were still concerned about diluting their ARPU, KDDI viewed their already-built network as sunk cost and was looking at adding more nodes to the network, even if they brought minimal revenue at first, since the acquisition and churn costs associated with machines were also a fraction of those associated with consumers. Over the past five years this thinking has spread to U.S. and European carriers. In 2011, U.S. carriers for the first time had specific quotas for M2M connections for their salespeople; those goals gave M2M adoption a significant boost.

According to Bill Davidson, "The thought of enabling a bunch of machines on the network when operators were struggling with capacity in their spectrum in large cities was not very popular. But later, I think, the broad deployment of 3G and now LTE come in as a hotspot of technology to offload traffic in areas where the networks were congested. I think that's given carriers a comfort level to address the potential growth in M2M."

The introduction of Amazon's Kindle in 2007 and the iPhone the same year did a lot for the broad awareness of what was possible. Kindle, in particular, demonstrated the power of subsidized connectivity costs. Says Peggy Smedley, "AT&T really got excited about it when they saw what the Kindle could do." Glen Allmendinger adds, "Of course, in many respects, with the advent of the smartphone, so much of what was already possible became so much more visible to so many more people. That whole connective phenomenon became so much clearer."

Steve Pazol concurs, "I think when Amazon's Kindle came along, that was the use case that let people say, 'Hey, I can actually literally change my business model by bringing a connected product to market.' That to me was the most concrete thing, that people could actually get it and say, 'Oh, I want to Kindle-ize my business.'"

The level of growing awareness is also highlighted by myriad studies and articles that have been published in the past few years: in 2011, *More Than 50 Billion Connected Devices*, a white paper by Ericsson;[7] and "The Second Economy" by W. Brian Arthur in the *McKinsey Quarterly*;[8] and in 2012, *Rise of the Machines* from the Economist Intelligence Unit, sponsored by SAP,[9] and *Industrial Internet*, a white paper from GE,[10] to name just a few.

The activity in the press and discussions about the Internet of Things are clear signs that it's not just hype and we are at a turning point. Bill Davidson predicts that as computing becomes embedded into more things, it will drive people's

---

[7] Ericsson, *More Than 50 Billion Connected Devices* (February 2011). http://www.ericsson.com/res/docs/whitepapers/wp-50-billions.pdf.

[8] W. Brian Arthur, "The second economy," *McKinsey Quarterly*, October 2011. http://www.mckinsey.com/insights/strategy/the_second_economy.

[9] The Economist Intelligence Unit Limited, *Rise of the machines. Moving from hype to reality in the burgeoning market for machine-to-machine communication* (2012). http://digitalresearch.eiu.com/m2m/.

[10] Peter C. Evans and Marco Annunziata, *Industrial Internet: Pushing the Boundaries of Minds and Machines*, General Electric (November 26, 2012). http://www.ge.com/docs/chapters/Industrial_Internet.pdf.

imaginations as to the types of information that can be extracted in real time.

Up until now, things like remote asset monitoring were more of a niche business. But increasing awareness, the availability of networks and equipment, and the sinking costs of electronics and network connectivity are driving huge economic activity. Bill Davidson recalls the issue with costs in the early days:

> I think the problem we had back then was the hardware cost. It was not efficient enough to get down to the price point that we needed to hit. Back in those days, I remember we put in our first large order for air cards [wireless modules]. I think I ordered fifteen hundred of them and because of that we got a price of $900 per module instead of $1,400."

Today, cellular wireless modules cost less than $20 apiece and the price is still going down.

Says Steve Pazol:

> As the networks get more pervasive, as processing power has gotten cheaper and as wireless standards are now in place, all of a sudden there is a mass capability to wirelessly enable things. A lot of that is riding on top of infrastructure and investment that was put in place earlier, both for the Internet and the cellular and the wireless communities.

The numbers speak for themselves. Glenn Lurie of AT&T is observing the dramatic growth of M2M users already:

We believe in it because, speaking for AT&T, I got sixteen million subscribers paying me for it today. We've been seeing significant growth for the last three years. I still believe we're just seeing the beginning of it. We're seeing the fruits of our labor that we put in for the last two years now. . . .

I think the biggest change in the last two years is that carriers with very, very large enterprise sales forces have decided that they are going to start marketing M2M. And having five thousand to eight thousand business-to-business salespeople in the U.S. talking about M2M causes the awareness to grow.

The resulting activity from carriers' customers is also very encouraging. As Glenn Lurie points out:

If you look at the consumers or small, medium, or large business players, their expectations have changed. Their expectations with the growth of smartphones and the iPhone and everything else is that all these devices are going to give me anytime, anywhere connectivity so I can use that device when and how I wanted to use it. So the customers are asking for it now; we're getting feedback from them. . . .

All the stars are aligned for us in that the modules that wirelessly enable these things have come down in price. The networks are there to support these and all the economics are coming into an alignment so that it makes sense to have these devices connected.

Glen Allmendinger observes:

> If you look at the last two years and you took the facilities culture as an example, we have a client in Dubai now that's got sixty thousand buildings where they're monitoring life safety equipment in all sixty thousand of them, and the outbound connectivity of the building is now cellular. If you'd gone and talked to typical engineers or architecture firms, even three years ago, four years ago, and talked about the use of cellular wireless in buildings, they would laugh at you. These things are starting to just go into each other. You have stories that instead of fighting all the cultural hurdles of trying to get into the IT firewalls and get that organized, they just slap the cellular thing on the side of the machine and put the signal out around the IT prison, if you will. If all of these pieces start intermingling in terms of common connectivity technologies, the traditional walls that had divided those cultures are finally crumbling.

John Major of Broadcom makes these observations about increasing simplicity of use:

> It's affordable. It's starting to work. It was nightmarishly difficult to do simple things. Take the early HP wireless printers: Hooking one of those up was a one-day project. Now, I think part of it is, it finally works. Stars are aligning.

Of course, there are still multiple challenges in getting M2M products to market, and we will review them in detail in chapter 6. But, as we see, the momentum is definitely building around the Internet of Things.

Would we allow the machines around us to take more control of our lives? Sanjay Sarma sees it this way:

> I think it will happen slowly and naturally, but what will happen is we will give up more and more things to automation. When we see the value of it, we'll get used to it. There are all sorts of anxieties, but then I realized that, for example, the lights in my house are motion triggered, the lights in my office are motion triggered, and they have been motion triggered for ten years. I don't ask for it, I don't get worried about it. So I guess my point is that I think it will happen. I just feel that this concept of having the environment adapt around you makes the cloud more like a living thing. There is a spooky edge to it, but I think we will get used to it.

The Internet of Things is becoming personable, something people on the street can relate to. Just recently, many people treated M2M as something "out there," not particularly big or compelling. Who really cares about monitoring industrial machines, towers, or lights, except their immediate stakeholders? However, M2M is also about improving health care (for example, automatically monitoring sugar levels or releasing insulin at the right times for diabetic patients, or helping people lose weight) and helping people manage their homes and families better (such as saving water, saving electricity, or reducing distracted driving).

Also, companies are starting to understand the value of mining usage data. For example, an electric tools company can benefit dramatically from knowing how its buyers are using its products, and build better products as a result.

Says Glen Allmendinger:

> Once people started to understand how much value was locked up in just understanding asset information, they realized how much money could be made. Awareness is kind of a consumer thing—the smartphone and the physical B2B [business-to-business] space, big asset management. I think those two worlds finally met and everybody kind of said, "Oh, I can do a lot with this." The more it seeps into stories like smart grids or health care, the more the subject becomes grounded in the context where people can imagine that there really are tangible advantages to trying to figure out what to do with all that data. Once the smartphone came into existence, all these sort of asset device stories that were roaming around got nearer to the consumer or user value, and all of a sudden, any person on the street could see that there are lots of things to be derived from location-based service: asset information, things in real time, essentially, and things that are state-based.

Peggy Smedley adds, "We have only just begun to see [M2M's] capabilities. Tech providers are just beginning to see what they can do with it. That's what makes it so appealing and so exciting."

We started this chapter by talking about exponential growth and the difficulties in predicting a market that will experience that kind of growth, using a chessboard as an example. However, in real life there is no end to the chessboard, and we don't really know how close to the middle we are. In the *McKinsey Quarterly* article "The Second Economy," W. Brian Arthur states, "There's no upper limit to this, no place where it has to end. . . . It would be easy to underestimate the degree to which this is going to make a difference."[11]

There have been many bold predictions of specific numbers the Internet of Things is going to reach. Ericsson predicts more than fifty billion devices by 2020 in "More Than Fifty Billion Connected Devices." GE predicts that "by 2025 it could be applicable to $82 trillion of output or approximately one half of the global economy."[12] It's hard to tell if these numbers are too high or too low. Mark Weiser saw a potential for hundreds of connected computers in every room, back in the '90s. That could put Ericsson's predictions to shame: "Once open connectivity interfaces are in place, service innovation will follow. There will be a shift from asking, 'Do we need to connect it?' to, 'What can we do differently now that it's connected?'"[13]

One of the most difficult things to foresee in business is timing—it's hard to tell how soon we are going to solve all the technical, operational, and behavioral problems to fully real-ize the Internet of Things vision. However, there is so much movement in this industry right now and many companies are reaping significant economic benefits today. The space is ripe for further innovation and experimentation because it offers specific opportunities to be realized in the short term.

In the following chapters we will look at specific examples and companies. We will also continue our discussions with industry experts about what is happening, what might hap-pen, and what needs to happen to bring about the vision of the Internet of Things.

---

[11] W. Brian Arthur, "The Second Economy," *McKinsey Quarterly* (2011), p.6.
[12] Evans and Annunziata, *Industrial Internet*, p.4.
[13] Ericsson, "More Than 50 Billion Connected Devices," p.4.

Chapter 2
TECHNOLOGY ECOSYSTEM

Technology is nothing. What's important is that you have a faith in people, that they're basically good and smart, and if you give them tools, they'll do wonderful things with them.

~ Steve Jobs

The Greek word *techne*, which is at the root of the word *technology*, means an art that has a practical application. Indeed, in the world of M2M technology, where things are being created as we write, there is as much art as there is science. For example, ask any radio frequency (RF) engineer about designing antennas for small, connected devices, and they will tell you it truly is an art in itself. Also, the state of the whole ecosystem in M2M resembles a living and growing organism where things often change, standards are being defined, and solutions are being figured out on the fly by people who to a certain extent resemble artists, even though most of them have engineering degrees.

The M2M technology ecosystem seems complex and confusing to many, especially if they are not on the technology side. But even for technologists, putting together bits and pieces to create a solution is often a daunting task. Many times, it's unclear where to look for those solutions.

In addition, as we mentioned in the previous chapter, the success of the Internet of Things largely depends on various industries embracing M2M technologies to solve their business problems. In this chapter, we present the parts of the technology ecosystem and its challenges, players, and future direction.

Overall, the M2M technology ecosystem can be split into three major groups: data acquisition, data transport, and data analysis.

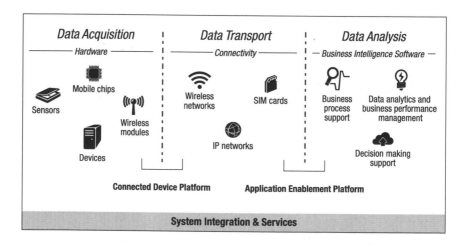

Data acquisition is the device or hardware space—this is where data is being collected from various sensors and sent to the network. Examples are body sensors that measure pulse or calorie consumption, automotive OBD-II[14] devices that measure car acceleration, and many others. RFID tags and readers belong to this category as well. To transmit data, devices are equipped with a radio transmitter, which can be cellular, Wi-Fi, or short range. After the data is collected, it is sent over a network; this is data transport. A network can be either wireless or wired, but for the purpose of this book we are going to primarily talk about wireless networks such as cellular, satellite, Wi-Fi for wide-range communication, and Bluetooth, ZigBee, and RFID for short-range communication.

Cellular networks are playing an increasingly important role in the M2M space, because the cost of mobile data is continually going down and because they provide the type of ubiquity that no other network can provide.

Data analysis is where the information that is collected from sensors and devices and transported over the network is being analyzed, interpreted, and acted upon or presented to humans to act upon. This area is gaining strong momentum because big data and real-time analytics are rapidly becoming core areas of differentiation for many companies. Connected devices are feeding these systems with data to improve tracking and tracing capabilities, optimize workflows, and automate systems.

The major innovation that has radically changed the data analysis space is a new kind of architecture, software, and

---

[14] OBD-II is the most common specification for On-Board Diagnostics. OBD is an automotive term referring to a vehicle's self-diagnostic and reporting capability. OBD systems give the vehicle owner or a repair technician access to information for various vehicle subsystems. Modern OBD implementations use a standardized digital communications port to provide real-time data, in addition to a standardized series of diagnostic trouble codes, or DTCs, which allow one to identify and remedy malfunctions within the vehicle. (Source: http://en.wikipedia.org/wiki/OBD-II#OBD-II.)

hardware that addresses the previous challenge of large data sets and how to capture, curate, store, search, analyze, and visualize all that data. Through technology innovation, working with huge data sets has become extremely affordable, compared to the realities of a couple of years ago. This enables us to find correlations, spot business trends, detect and prevent potential criminal activity, or optimize workflows of all kinds.

To ensure the smooth flow of data, there are platforms that enable communications between any two of the three major groups in the technology ecosystem. For example, between data acquisition and data transport there is a Connected Device Platform (CDP). The CDP, sometimes referred to as *middleware*, ensures that the devices and sensors can be easily connected, primarily to a cellular network, and that the devices can be remotely managed. Imagine trying to reset thousands or hundreds of thousands of devices manually in the field. This is just one example of a nightmare that a CDP is supposed to prevent.

Because the management of sometimes millions of devices (activation, deactivation, tracking, roaming, etc.) is very complex, carriers use CDPs like Jasper Wireless to try to build custom solutions, or form alliances to build proprietary platforms at scale. Roaming is a critical function for many M2M solutions; therefore, we mostly see large global carriers that operate in a number of countries playing the most active role as M2M connectivity providers.

Between data transport and data analysis there is an Application Enablement Platform (AEP). The AEP allows developers to produce applications that run using the data from connected devices. For example, an AEP will have well-defined APIs (Application Programming Interfaces) to the devices in the field. Through these APIs it is possible to access device sensor data, its location, battery level, and many other parameters. Using this information, a developer can, for example, create a new application to track valuable cargo, its location, and temperature.

Some of the challenges the application developers are facing in the M2M space revolve around mobility. In the cellular world, where the bandwidth is scarce and relatively expensive in large volumes, it is crucial to use it efficiently. In most cases this implies making the device smarter so it can decide whether or not to send data back to the cloud.

Says Steve Pazol:

> I think the biggest challenge is that a lot of the people building the applications don't know anything about wireless. They might be experts in medical devices, but they're not experts in how to build a device and how to write software that functions effectively over a [cellular] network.

Bill Davidson adds:

> You have sensors collecting data. The question is how much of it ends up needing to be transmitted? If I am in a health care application and if my sensor is looking at certain vital signs, as long as they are okay, I don't have to transmit anything. One of the key things we are facing right now is developers have to start worrying about how to build their apps efficiently. I think that is why we have seen the mobile operators go away from fixed pricing for a little while. I think they want to instill the sense of efficiency in the developer community. When they had a fixed price for unlimited mobile data, nobody had to worry about being efficient; it did not matter

if the app checked the status of a device every ten seconds.

Let's take a closer look at the M2M technology ecosystem and its parts.

Device hardware (data acquisition) is one of the most challenging areas of the ecosystem, primarily because it comes in all sizes and colors. You may think of black box–type devices that are usually installed on industrial equipment, but there are also OBD-II devices that get installed in cars, elegant body-worn fitness devices, connectivity modules that get embedded in home appliances, moisture sensors that go in the soil, RFID readers, and so on. All require different form factors, different types of connectivity, and different applications.

Here's what Steve Pazol has to say about hardware:

> I think it really comes down to the ability to embed connectivity and get those things to market easier and faster, without taking a year. That's the long pole on the tent, and it is on the device side. It's normally not on the software side or on the connectivity side; it is, how do I get that device manufactured to scale and be able to update it over the Internet and do those kinds of things? That's the biggest area for improvement that will really get more products to market easier and faster.

For example, a big part of hardware design is electrical design, which defines all the electrical and electronic components that live under the hood.

One of the most critical parts of the electrical design is antenna design. The improvements in antenna design over the past twenty years have been truly amazing. Some of us remember the early cell phones with pullout antennas. Over time, antennae became hidden inside the actual device, and later antennae have been integrated into the bodies of smartphones. In the meantime, devices got much smaller and complex as more and more antennae had to be integrated within the same small footprint.

For example, an average smartphone today must have antennae supporting the following radio frequencies: CDMA, GSM, UMTS, LTE, GPS, and Bluetooth. Imagine all these technologies embedded into tiny body-worn devices or consumer electronics! Just imagine wearable devices like watches, ankle bracelets, belt buckles, glucose meters, insulin pumps, and heart monitors. With such a rich variety, antenna design will remain more art than science for the foreseeable future, until some new semistandardized approach to design is found.

As we have seen with many consumer devices, the right design can be the most important factor for market success. In the case of wireless devices, the design complexity increases due to the constraints of the actual electronic components and antennae, as well as the battery. When we talk about consumer body-worn devices there are certain things that have to be guaranteed besides nice look and feel. There are certain regulations about SAR (radiation absorption), which directly depend on antenna performance, and if a device does not meet these, the FCC and wireless carriers won't certify it and retailers won't be allowed to sell it.

Heat is an important factor that is highly regulated—the device can't get too hot to be worn on the body. In addition, the battery should be just the right size so it provides sufficient power for a long enough period (it's doubtful consumers will want to charge all their body-worn devices as often as they charge their cell phones—several weeks or months of battery life would make more sense). The device also has to be small enough to fit into a nicely designed consumer electronics piece.

To summarize, these hardware design challenges offer significant opportunities for companies willing to build reference designs and develop hardware platforms that would fit various markets and form factors.

When we look at the device software side of things, integration of sensors is becoming extremely crucial. Here is where contextual intelligence comes into play. Sensors will play an even more prominent role with the proliferation of the Internet of Things. Google Now is a great example of how powerful contextual intelligence can be. The concept behind Google Now can be applied to all kinds of contextual data: Sensor data that delivers information such as location, acceleration, barometric pressure, light, and temperature can be used to build predictive models, which then reduce the need for always-on, real-time data transmission, which in turn reduce the cost of data transmission and improve battery life.

Wireless devices solve one problem but create another. Removing all cables from the device allows for easy installation. But in most cases, a device needs to have autonomous power in the form of a battery as well. In many real-life use cases, that battery would need to last a long time—weeks, months, or years, depending on the use. There are many ways to extend battery life today. One way is to put the device in a sleeping mode when it's not transmitting data. Another way is to harvest energy from solar, wind, vibration, heat, or other alternative sources that exist where the device is in use. For example, using human body heat as a source of energy for wireless devices seems like a lucrative concept. Today, just enough electricity can be harvested from human body heat to power a simple sensor, but there's not enough to power full-blown cellular devices. But perhaps in the future, as technology improves, there will be ways to do just that.

For some applications, often there is no dedicated communication device, but smartphones are used as a hub for wireless sensors. For example, BodyMedia's body-worn sensor communicates over Bluetooth with a smartphone, and the smartphone sends the data to the cloud. We will evaluate the pros and cons of this approach in subsequent chapters.

As for data transport, one can only imagine what kind of impact M2M devices will have on cellular networks, especially if they reach the quantity of fifty billion predicted by Ericsson.

We had lunch with a group of tech professionals, one of whom was working on a project to estimate the data usage impact for mobile carriers over the next three to five years. After he described his calculation model, we asked him if he had considered other devices, besides smartphones and tablets. He asked us which devices we meant, and we suggested electric meters, monitoring devices, personal fitness devices, heart monitors, glucose meters, insulin pumps, personal tracking devices, and so on. He told us no, the model only included smartphones and tablets, and we were surprised by this.

It is highly likely that the volume of data generated by these *other* devices will dramatically exceed the volume generated by smartphones and tablets. While we are going to be watching high-definition videos on our tablets, all these devices are going to be quietly sending alerts, syncing data, and requesting status updates, which in aggregate will amount to terabytes of data. At the very least, these amounts will be comparable to those generated by smartphones, laptops, and tablets. What implications will this have on carriers' networks? How can one build an accurate forecasting model for data volumes without taking into account other devices or the Internet of Things?

As with any forecasting model, it's difficult to make linear predictions in an extremely nonlinear world. However, one thing is certain: The data traffic of non-cellphone devices has huge potential and will most likely put a significant strain on wireless carrier networks. As usual, the main players will have to adapt and adjust as things move along, but being prepared for a large upswing in network data traffic will separate the leaders from the followers.

Having global access is also critical, because no OEM would want to build different versions of devices for various markets or put different SIM cards into the devices depending on which regional markets they go to. Says Glenn Lurie of AT&T:

> Since the very first meeting I've ever had with the very first customer I ever talked about multiple years ago, one of the very first questions was: Can you support us for a global launch? It used to be a very, very difficult thing to deliver a single SIM. Now, you put the same SIM in every single device you build and you have one carrier to work with to have coverage in two hundred countries around the world. So the single SIM simplifies device manufacturing, the single SIM allows you to ship that automotive device anywhere you want to go, and when it lands it gets turned on automatically.

On the data analysis side of things, one of the major trends is Software as a Service, or SaaS, provided over the cloud. This means that in many cases, M2M solutions don't have to be integrated into the Enterprise Resource Planning (ERP) system right away. Employees and management can access the data in the cloud from their desktops, laptops, tablets, and smartphones.

As we have recently seen, IT departments cannot keep up with the innovation happening in the marketplace that is provided by new SaaS companies and application start-ups. Even large players in this space are actively acquiring small companies for their big data expertise. There are many examples of consumer productivity apps that are much more effective than the ones provided and integrated by IT departments. When it comes to business applications such as asset tracking, many companies are offering tracking services over the Web from the cloud. Today most businesses are comfortable with the idea of the enterprise data being handled by third parties in the cloud, which was not the case just a few years ago.

Many companies are actively using cloud services. However, at some point, integration with the existing software systems in the enterprise, such as ERP, will become an issue. From a provider standpoint, it will be crucial to first provide the necessary functionality from the cloud and have open APIs to enable easy integration into the existing enterprise software systems.

While there are a lot of things that have already happened to simplify and enable the Internet of Things, a lot of things still need to happen. Among those things are integration, standardization, simplification, what to do with all the data produced by all the devices and sensors, and how to turn that data into knowledge so it can affect decisions and processes within companies, to support and improve existing processes. Steve Pazol shares the following thoughts on the data analytics potential:

> I think right now people are just putting in the infrastructure. I don't think people have figured out, in many cases, what to do with the data. Maybe they understand the primary use of the data: By monitoring a truck location I can increase my supply chain efficiency. Maybe there are other uses of that data—secondary, tertiary uses of that data—and there is additional value. I don't think the big data concepts and the analytics concepts have really been

applied to M2M yet. Maybe in certain domains or certain specific applications, but I think there's a lot of opportunity, I mean a ton of opportunity there. I think on the software business analytics, it becomes easier and easier to build applications.

To me, at the end of the day, M2M is really about data. You're getting data off devices or sensors that have been hard to get, but once it's in the cloud, it's data. So all the data tools, if it's big data or any kind of business intelligence software, all that stuff is applicable to it. So I think just the same tools and technologies, like Google or Facebook, really do a lot of analytics on their users, and the amount of data that they have, they're very applicable into the M2M space.

When deciding on which networks to run an M2M solution, we would like to point out the ubiquity versus granularity problem. For example, RFID tags are very low cost, don't need a battery, and have an infinite life. One can put an RFID tag on almost anything—for instance, every item in a grocery store. That way, RFID provides a high level of granularity for seeing and detecting things. However, for each RFID installation there needs to be RFID readers, which require installation, calibration, and fine-tuning. The RFID does not provide the ubiquity of other networks. Let's take cellular: Mobile carriers provide access to cellular networks almost everywhere—cellular networks are ubiquitous. However, the cellular devices are costly compared to the RFID tags, they are bulky, and they require batteries to run. Cellular devices do not offer the same level of granularity that RFID provides.

To better understand this problem, we spoke with Professor Sanjay Sarma of MIT. Sanjay pointed out that the biggest cost in RFID today is in installation and integration. One way to address the issue of ubiquity, he says, would be to wirelessly enable RFID readers with 4G or Wi-Fi and make them ubiquitous. Sanjay says, "Imagine if the reader comes with a standard electric plug, all you need to do is plug it in and you're good to go." He envisions the time when so many devices are going to have RFID-reader capability that it will solve the problem of the short range of RFID devices—there will always be a reader in range.

On the other side, mobile carriers are just starting to embrace Wi-Fi services as an offering on top of their cellular networks, but it's possible to imagine a not-too-distant future where mobile carriers will be selling high-bandwidth wireless access to the Internet regardless of technology. This would partially solve the problem of ubiquity of various types of wireless networks.

All in all, wireless networks are a very important consideration when building an M2M business. Depending on the individual use case, M2M modules have to be able to receive satellite signals in remote areas, or use Bluetooth or Near-Field Communication (NFC) for short distances. Telecom carrier networks and GPS are by far the most dominant modes of transmission; however, in high-security environments one might opt for NFC as the transmission standard. Sensor-based networks that rely on a number of factors, such as exact location or temperature, often use a combination of available wireless networks to provide precise and accurate data.

When looking at key players, their positioning, and potential profit pools in the near future, it is important to understand each player's unique position in the market, potential external effects on the supply and demand side, new players that are entering the market, and potential disruption that may change the overall industry dynamic or allow for alternative approaches and solutions that have not been feasible before.

Each of the players in the value chain has a chance to improve their competitive positioning by building a unique offering. Commoditization will happen where there is lots of competition and no differentiation.

Applying these principles to the M2M market, one can assume the largest profit pools are expected in the hardware, solution design, and data analytics spaces. Why would that be? Because although there's a common perception that it's hard to make money with hardware, we believe that in M2M there are still a lot of opportunities to reap benefits from hardware. First of all, complexity is one of the key reasons the market has not taken off as expected. Most complexity in M2M today is in devices, but if one could remove this complexity, significant value could be unleashed for everyone in the ecosystem.

If we separate device providers into chipset vendors, wireless module providers, and complete device vendors/ integrators, we believe the chip vendors and the final device vendors/integrators are where the most innovation will happen in the coming years, which will lead to big benefits for the most successful players. Wireless module providers, however, will see strong price competition, and some of them will most likely be squeezed out of the market. The market is waiting for a player (or several players) that can solve the hardware scalability problem in M2M. Companies that excel in this space will do well.

Today, most M2M device providers reuse existing chipsets from the cellular world because they present huge economies of scale, considering the overhead spread over billions of chips. For this reason, key chipset players are unlikely to develop super-low-cost dedicated chipsets for M2M as long as this market stays relatively small from their point of view—that is, compared to their core cellular business. This situation offers a great opportunity for disruption, and some new market entrants might come up with a completely new approach that revolutionizes this market.

On the other end of the supply chain are software and application platforms. This market is still highly fragmented and allows for high margins for system integrators, making many business cases less attractive than they could be. This market always reminds us of the mobile phone industry in the early days and the fragmentation issues that there were for a number of years. If a couple of players are able to design application platforms that allow for easy and cost-effective development and deployment of applications, these platforms would be able to benefit from massive network effects, like the ones we have seen around mobile platforms starting in 2006.

Also, data analysis and workflow optimization will be an interesting growth market going forward. Because these markets are still immature at this point, companies that are able to become central market players will have a very attractive position.

The last segment to be mentioned is end-to-end solutions providers. Being able to take the complexity out of solution design and become a comprehensive one-stop shop will be an attractive proposition for technology companies and system integrators.

The core growth drivers for the industry will be new services propelled by a strong reduction of overall costs throughout the supply chain. Many services today are custom built, and the lack of standards and platforms leads to costly development by system integrators. Imagine a world with two or three powerful application development platforms in combination with a massive uptake of B2B and B2C use cases. This would lead to a powerful shift of attention and investment in this field and most likely trigger exponential growth of the whole business vertical.

By far the largest barrier for growth today is the complexity of the value chain, in combination with a lack of standardized platforms. This issue creates a major entry barrier for smaller players, who typically avoid the complex certification processes. Once this process becomes easier to handle, in combination with reduced development costs for applications, one can imagine an uptake similar to what we have seen on iOS and Android in the past few years.

If we look further into the future, it becomes apparent that the existing data infrastructure is not ready for the exponential growth of the Internet of Things and will have to adjust and adapt. Glen Allmendinger of Harbor Research believes peer-to-peer among M2M devices will eventually become the default architecture standard for the Internet of Things, and the networks will become much less hierarchical than in the past. He also believes we will see a radically different definition of servers, devices, routers, and hubs in this space going forward.

Assaf Biderman of MIT also believes that today's Web is just not built for M2M services. As vendors start opening APIs on their devices for anyone to write applications using device sensors, and as security is added to all connections, a new approach will be needed.

Peggy Smedley brings a great perspective from beyond the tech world:

> In this digital transformation, everybody has to work together. It's not one company or one player that's going to do it. I think the world of M2M is a technology tapestry of creating useful solutions that are going to continue to emerge. Most consumers are not going to want to know what's going on behind the scenes. Just like with cell phones, we really don't care how it works; we just want to know that it's working all the time. And I think the same applies to M2M—we really don't want to know how it's all

happening, but we want to know that technology
is constantly advancing.

In this chapter we gave a high-level overview of the M2M
technology ecosystem as it is today—a living organism—with
thousands of people coming up with new solutions to complex
problems and almost creating art in the process.

Chapter 3
THE FUTURE OF THE SILENT INTELLIGENCE

*Business is going to change more in the next
ten years than it has in the last fifty.*

~ Bill Gates

We made a point in chapter 1 that the exponential growth of the Internet of Things is going to have a profound effect on our lives over the next five to ten years. If we are correct, the quote above that opens Bill Gates's book *Business @ the Speed of Thought: Succeeding in the Digital Economy,*[15] written over a decade ago, seems to be more relevant today than ever.

However, we decided to start this chapter with a provocative question: Will humans ever become a decision bottleneck in the

---

[15] Bill Gates, *Business @ the Speed of Thought: Succeeding in the Digital Economy* (New York: Grand Central Publishing, 1999).

Internet of Things? Considering how much decision-making ability has already been given to machines and how much more is going to go that way, and considering the speed at which information flows from sensors and devices to the cloud, will humans be able to comprehend? Are humans the major limiting factor in the development of the Internet of Things today? And, more importantly, will humans be able to cope with all this information?

When we spoke with Astro Teller of Google, he reminded us of an interesting story. In 2005, there was a freestyle chess tournament hosted by the website PlayChess.com. "Freestyle" meant any humans or computers, or any combination of humans and computers, could participate in the tournament. Who do you think won? One would expect a grand master or a supercomputer, or perhaps a grand master with an average computer, or an amateur with a supercomputer. One would hardly expect a couple of amateurs with laptops to win a global chess tournament.

But in fact, that's exactly what happened. Two American amateurs, Zackary Stephen and Steven Cramton, playing under the name ZackS with ordinary computers, won the tournament. It was quite a shock for all the participants.

Analyzing what happened, Garry Kasparov wrote in *Chess 2.0* and later in the article *The Chess Master and the Computer* that the winners used the computers to calculate tactical moves and avoid simple blunders, while they concentrated on planning the strategy of the games. Garry concluded, "[W]eak human + machine + better process was superior to a strong computer alone and, more remarkably, superior to a strong human + machine + inferior process."[16]

---

[16] Garry Kasparov, "New in Chess," *Chess 2.0*, May 2005. Also Garry Kasparov, "The Chess Master and the Computer," *New York Review of Books*, February 11, 2010. http://www.nybooks.com/articles/archives/2010/feb/11/the-chess-master-and-the-computer/.

That combination appears to be unbeatable, and humans have demonstrated a capacity for adapting new tools of increasing complexity to excel and prosper. More importantly, human creativity seems to have no limit; as new technologies and possibilities emerge, humans will identify new problems to be solved or new ways of solving old problems, like in the chess example.

The notion of removing humans from the equation and delegating more decision-making to machines is nothing new. Manufacturing is one example of an area where things started moving much faster than human speed long ago. Machines are often not only faster than humans, but also more accurate, and they dramatically minimize the chance of human error caused by fatigue. As things around us become smarter due to remotely controlled sensors, machines will take over more and more tasks.

One of the amazing things coming down the pipeline is the self-driving car. Says Astro Teller:

> Self-driving cars in the not-too-distant future are just going to be meaningfully better than people. It will become irresponsible and antiquated for people to drive cars. That is absolutely going to happen in the next decade. I believe that very strongly. Whether Google does it or not, reasonable people could disagree, but whether that generally is going to happen, that I feel very strongly about.

In reality, the Google-X driverless car project has demonstrated that autonomous cars can already navigate traffic and follow the speed limit.

And that's just the tip of the proverbial iceberg. Air traffic control might be another area to see more automation soon, as planes learn to communicate better with the ground and with each other, avoiding humans in the process. Astro says, "I bet you there are a lot of places where that's going to be one of the big pieces of news—the radically changing rhythms, styles, interaction modalities between people and computers for solving hard, big, distributed problems."

By the same token, we can think of self-tuning machines, which use sensor information and information from the cloud to upgrade themselves, fine-tune themselves, calibrate themselves, and so on. This is already happening with our computers and smartphones that keep themselves up-to-date, almost without the need for a manual upgrade. It's also starting to happen with Machine-to-Machine devices. For example, Tesla, the electric car made in California, is equipped with a cellular module, which enables the driver to always have the latest firmware over the air. Today, the user still has to manually initiate the upgrade, but in the future the car may take care of it by itself.

As machines become smarter and require less human intervention, it will have a significant impact on productivity. Says Steve Pazol about equipment servicing businesses:

> Historically, if it was manual, one person could only handle sixty sites a month—every half a day they would go to a new site. Well, if I'm connected to those sites and I can basically be on-site by not having to go anywhere, I might be able to have one person manage three hundred sites. Only when there's a real problem would you have to go to that site or dispatch a specialist or a local person, and that would also generate better customer service. As you start moving up that curve, I think it provides better customer service; it's actually cheaper to deploy M2M for the manufacturer.

This development will also have an impact on jobs. But as the number of traditional technician jobs may decline, new jobs are going to be created. For example, better information and forecasting can help optimize cyclical industries and enable them to better manage downturns.

Peggy Smedley also believes machines are going to make an increasing number of decisions:

> The applications become more and more sophisticated and users will be reporting increasingly complex interactions over time. In many cases consumers and businesses alike will be removed from the equation. That's what's going to happen. Given defined and controlled parameters, machines will be making a lot of the decisions.

As things evolve and we learn to collect and analyze the information from multiple sources to give us a better picture, we will see the emergence of total asset management, for example, by combining RFID, RTLS (real-time location systems), cellular, and satellite communication: If I load a box of high-value pharmaceuticals, equipped with RFID, onto a container, which in turn is put on a train, which is later put on a boat, I can potentially track the pharmaceuticals in real time by tracking the container, the train, and the boat, as long as I know which container, train, or boat my box is associated with.

We could track a FedEx package in real time much better than we can today, when it only gives us milestone updates. A FedEx package will become a smart package and will know not only its location at any given time, but also if it's running late and if the contents of the package are safe by collecting contextual information about the package.

A lot of contextual information is also collected from body-worn devices like Fitbit and BodyMedia. Today, by using movement patterns, body heat, and heart rate from its various sensors, a BodyMedia device is able to tell if a person is in a car or exercising on a bike. As more sensors become available and more information can be processed and analyzed, it will be possible to tell more about individual behavior. Astro Teller says, "We could see things about people's commute cycles, about how long they commute and how it relates to their sleep and other things. No one has ever seen things like this on a hundred people or even on a million people."

But at the end of the day, there needs to be a good use case. We will talk more about use cases in subsequent chapters.

Christian Busch says, "I don't think certain things will come just because they are technically possible. I still think that the killer use case for consumer M2M is still out there."

We had a very interesting conversation with Dr. Sanjay Sarma of MIT about his concept of cloud cars and cloud avatars, and he said:

> We all accept that the connectivity across entities is inevitable. My cell phone should be able to talk to my car, my car should be able to talk to my home, and so on. The problem is how. Most people don't know how to pair their Bluetooth. They don't know how to pair their printers to their computers. It's a pain. I like to believe that the shortest path between my computer at home and my printer at home might not be a straight line between the computer and the printer but may actually be through the cloud. The idea is that it's easier for me to access my computer in the cloud and have my . . . computer avatar talk in the cloud to my printer avatar. If you get into that

thinking about things, it's like the continuation of a Second Life[17] concept.

We find this a very compelling vision, one that would allow anyone to look at any two devices in the cloud—through a browser or a dedicated app—draw a line between these two devices, and they would connect. They would figure out the protocol, they would find, download, and install the right firmware, if needed, and they would connect. All of this would happen seamlessly, without much user intervention. This logic can be applied to any home electronic device: televisions, computers, printers, and so on.

Sanjay continues:

> The paradigm we use becomes trivial: It's as simple as I cross a straight line on a browser, right? We can work to hook up my printer and boom—I'm ready to go. I should be able to drag a file from my computer to my printer or drag a scanned file from my printer on the cloud to my computer on the cloud. My computer is paired to Dropbox; it's paired to iCloud because I have a Mac. It's that easy. Then the cloud becomes a kind of one-stop shop to pair anything to anything. The basic principle is instead of having many-to-many connections, you have one-to-one connections to the cloud, and then you do the many-to-many connections in the cloud to make other things more manageable.

---

[17] *Second Life* is an online virtual world developed by Linden Lab. It was launched on June 23, 2003. A number of free client programs, or Viewers, enable Second Life users to interact with one another through avatars (also called Residents). (Source: http://en.wikipedia.org/wiki/Second_Life.)

As long as devices have clearly defined interfaces, this vision is possible and anything will be able to connect to anything else. Sanjay adds:

> At MIT we have a project called CloudCar. My car has an exact avatar in the cloud, and that is what I'm doing to my home. The idea is that I can lock and unlock my car remotely for my son, who is visiting and wants to drive the car. I can turn the engine on and off. I'm not that far away from essentially turning my car into the equivalent of Airbnb for cars. At Airbnb I can rent a room in someone's house if I want. The idea is to do the same with the car, especially if it is just sitting there and just costing money. People should be able to log in and borrow somebody's car, just pay twenty bucks and be done. They should be able to make it happen just using their cell phone."

As technology becomes available, we can see use cases like this gaining popularity in the future. However, this vision raises three points. First of all, somebody will need to figure out a way to make the whole process of finding and renting someone else's car simple. The second thing is the need for a paradigm shift in how people view their cars. For some, their car is a very personal thing, their fashion statement or status symbol, and not just a utility that can be shared with anybody else. The third area would be security; the idea that someone can hack into their car would scare most people away.

Sanjay Sarma used Airbnb.com as an example of how things that were almost unthinkable before can become big business and how what used to be a niche market went mainstream. Considering that a connected car, a CloudCar, can always be tracked with GPS, it's unlikely that it's going to be hijacked, or at least it can be quickly recovered if it is. There's probably a big enough market of people who would not mind renting out their car for some time to others.[18] Finally, the issue of security applies to all connected cars and homes and needs to be addressed.

But the concept of CloudCar goes much further. If I publish the APIs to my car, other services can subscribe to it with my permission. For example, a dealership or a service shop could subscribe to a stream of data coming off my car sensors in real time. In that case I might get a message from the shop that they determined that the oxygen sensor on my car isn't working very well; I might want to bring the car in. The service shop could look at my Google calendar, which I gave them access to, and say that if I drop it off by 3 p.m. on Friday they can replace the oxygen sensor within two hours. Adds Sanjay, "My point is that if my car is just sitting at home or sitting in the parking lot by itself, nothing is happening. But if it's continuously replicating itself in the cloud, then all these things become possible."

Many more things would become possible if the cloud knew the position of a car and its status. For example, road tolls could be collected virtually just by calculating the distance using the GPS data. There would be no need to construct costly toll-collection infrastructure. This way, things like toll collection would cease being a hardware thing and would become a software thing with all the benefits of software—lower costs, quicker upgrades, faster implementation, and ease of use. The last point is especially valid, because once hardware infrastructure is in place, it's much harder to make any changes if it

---

[18] Peer-to-peer car-sharing services like Getaround, JustShareIt, and others are in operation. We don't know if they'll be successful, but this type of service would not be possible without M2M.

proves to be user-unfriendly—it's much easier to tweak things with software.

That is probably one of the most exciting aspects of connected devices in the cloud—being able to quickly develop and deploy new services without the capital expenditure and installation time of hardware.

Car insurance can be paid based on the actual miles the car has been driven. This idea is already catching on with usage-based insurance popularized by Progressive. Parking can be measured and charged the same way, avoiding parking meters all together. Sanjay Sarma continues:

> If you think about it the way we are doing it today, I have all these toll passes in my car: I have MIT parking access, I have E-ZPass. I might have a Progressive Snapshot, my insurance download, which checks to see how my car is doing. I might have a LoJack app to follow my car if it gets lost. I may have something else to keep track of my kid, how fast and safe my teenager is driving. All that could be done with one little thing. Then we recognize that all you need is a clean platform on which people can run apps and all the other things become just things that dangle off one coat hook.

Sanjay also brought up an interesting vision of using the cloud model to minimize compromises in software and service development:

> For example, RFID tells the software system in logistics to move certain pallets onto that certain truck. The vision of RFID is that the world is talking back. As if to say, for example, "Hey, sorry,

the pallet didn't go on that truck; it went on the wrong truck." However, the fundamental assumption in the old legacy enterprise software systems in logistics companies is that the world does not talk back. There was just no way to do it. Your big computer system interface is assuming the world is not going to talk back to you, but the upcoming technology *lets* the world talk back to you. So what do you do? You replace the technology or you compromise the vision.

Each time new applications or new technologies face the old ones, there is a need to compromise by integrating them, looking for the lowest common denominator. But, according to Sanjay, we may not have to compromise much longer:

> Out of all these compromises, IT integration is a misnomer. What you're trying to do is deal with the compromises and write code to deal with the compromises. Fundamentally, I believe IT integration is going to disappear. What is going to happen though, I think, is that everything is going to go to a cloud, like a Salesforce.com model. Things are going to become much more standardized, much more like take it or leave it. People aren't going to use that device that is running a bad piece of software. There is going to be some very fundamental changes in the software world. Traditional software just can't handle it. What I say is forget it, don't try to integrate with traditional software systems. It's like carrying a Maserati on the back of a camel. What you want to do is think of it as if you are doing it from scratch, because in fact, the Internet of Things is not just

adding one percent of information, it's adding one
hundred times more information, so you might as
well design for that instead of inheriting the compromises of the previous generation, which means
go straight to the cloud, do stuff in all the ways you
and I would agree are modern.

We find this vision interesting and thought-provoking.
Already today we are seeing the signs with consumerization of
IT. Not only do employees bring their own devices to companies, they are using many cloud-based productivity tools like
Evernote and Dropbox, completely bypassing their IT departments. Teams collaborate using Asana, a cloud-based project
management software.

Most of the innovation is happening outside of corporate
IT departments. The role of the IT department gets reduced
to how they ensure the security and safety of the company's
proprietary information so that none of it gets shared with the
public. They also are looking for ways to integrate these new
cloud productivity tools, mostly developed by start-ups, with
their legacy systems, but it's very hard for them to keep up with
the speed of innovation that start-ups can provide.

Similar trends are happening with education. MITx, a
nonprofit organization sponsored by MIT and Harvard that
provides cloud-based learning, is a great example.

Because most innovation is already happening in the cloud,
we are seeing the same trend spreading to the Internet of Things.
For example, many real-time location services (RTLS) companies
provide their services in the cloud, bypassing the IT departments in hospitals. In our interviews with them, we consistently
heard that the less they deal with the IT departments within
hospitals, the faster and cheaper they can usually implement
their projects. Most companies providing asset tracking and

monitoring services do it in a SaaS way, again bypassing the IT departments and providing much more cost-effective and accurate solutions that way.

But speaking of security of connectivity and information, Sanjay Sarma believes cloud services are not any less secure than the ones provided by corporate IT:

> I think that outsourcing innovation actually ensures security, because you have a few professionals that have best practices. I'd rather trust a thousand people at a company like Amazon Web Services than the four guys in an IT division who have been working there for twenty years. The cloud companies will have the latest enterprise software on their machines, including the latest security updates. That is particularly true if you are doing certain things with sensors that would generate gazillions of terabytes, so much data to be interpreted, analyzed, etc.

Indeed, internal IT departments might not have capacity and capability to deal with these volumes of data.

While cloud services can ensure quick software development, deployment, and iterations in M2M, hardware remains a big bottleneck. The problem is fragmentation; for companies, it's hard to justify investing if they are only going to build thousands of devices of a particular kind, or even fifty thousand devices. Because many M2M use cases require custom hardware and it's not clear at the beginning how big a particular use case is going to be, things become costly and hard to iterate. We believe a lot of innovation is going to happen in the M2M hardware space in the next few years.

If we project into the future, we see very promising technologies that can do to hardware what cloud services did to software.

One is 3-D printing, which would allow quick building of prototypes in real time that could then be quickly field-tested. As 3-D printing evolves, we see even quick manufacturing of small batches of custom devices. While 3-D printing is an attractive concept for mechanical parts, interesting things are happening with electronic parts as well. A lot of innovation is happening with inorganic printed electronics. According to Sanjay Sarma, we are probably seven to ten years from being able to 3-D print electronics that will be used commercially in M2M devices.

The problem here is not just the complexity of electronic components like modems, processors, and memory chips; it's also scale: how to quickly move from on-demand printing of a small batch to commercial printing of millions of devices. We believe these problems are going to be successfully resolved in the coming years and we will witness a breakthrough in the M2M hardware space within the next few years.

Astro Teller believes the future of hardware in M2M is not going to be much different from what has happened in the past with PCs and mobile phones. He says:

> Of course it is much easier to scale software than to scale hardware. In the phone and in the PC space, there were a lot of different hardware manufacturers. We forget their names now, and most of them fell away because they could not scale. But at the time, it wasn't clear who was going to win. The reason that everyone is rolling their own hardware right now is not because they want to make hardware. You go up and down the valley here and you'll find twenty companies doing wearable body monitoring. They don't know anything about hardware. They don't even like hardware. It causes you to raise more money. If they could not do it, they would not do it.

As soon as the APIs from a few of the device manufacturers are good enough, you will see essentially
no more new entrants into the hardware market
unless someone has a radically good idea and wants
to be the best in the world of devices. All the new
entrants will start to be software-only entrants and
will ride on top of the existing hardware, and then
there will be a race between the fifty companies that
have something you can wear and, over time, all but
three or four of them will fall away, which is exactly
what happened to PCs. It's exactly what happened
with the phones. Maybe Jawbone will win. Maybe
it's Fitbit. Maybe it's BodyMedia.[19]

As Sanjay Sarma points out, there are still significant challenges today with the information infrastructure for the Internet
of Things, especially if we expect the data volumes to increase
a hundred-fold, if not more. Glen Allmendinger believes information brokerage is badly needed, before we agree on common
standards. As we start getting inputs from gazillions of sensors, systems need a way to recognize where the information is
coming from and what that information is. We need metadata.

For example, if I'm a third-party developer, I would like
to know that information from body monitors or all medical
devices is coded a certain way. Says Glen:

The problem is that there really is no information architecture standard out there just to make
it incredibly simplistic. The classic hurdle here
is as you move to that kind of distributed fluid

---

[19] After this interview and just before this book was published, BodyMedia
was acquired by Jawbone.

movement of information, you need some sort of dictionary to know that Smith Street in Pakistan means the same thing as Smith Street in Wyoming. It's a nomenclature/semantics issue. But all those kinds of information identifiers and things that create identity and things that create shared identity and things that create identity across very heterogeneous kinds of data, those are all huge hurdles. Draw a line in the sand and just simply say, assume we figure out how to solve that problem, we can all agree on a dictionary, then the next problem is interpretation and value metering. In other words, these are all real-time state-based systems we're talking about in the future, and the thing that's probably missing in this—and I don't know how best to describe it—is the brokerage layer that allows for people to essentially meter the value and meter the use of shared data. After I get the dictionary, I need the broker.

According to Kevin Ashton, dealing with the identity of things was the main reason for developing the Internet of Things vision and the RFID standards. Having universal code, which would enable objects in the physical world to report on what they are and what they do in a unified way, was the absolutely essential thing. The same concept needs to populate the world of the Internet of Things outside of RFID, like sensors and devices, which is expanding very rapidly. Also, considering that very soon the amount of data on the Internet produced by machines will supersede the amount of data created by humans, having the right interpretation algorithms is absolutely critical.

Glen Allmendinger continues:

If I can have a dictionary and a broker, then I can create huge amounts of residual values out of all of this data. In other words, if I go back to the power plugs on the wall example, I've got things like primary values where I can just turn energy on and off, or I can buy energy at a point in time. To the appliance maker, I can understand how many times a day, for example, single women between the ages of forty and fifty-five use their washing machines, right? In the hospital example, I can do things to optimize the user experiences of a patient as he passes through the hospital and touches multiple devices. There's a huge amount of data that could be shared that would allow all of that system to be so much more state-based and real-time aware, that it just naturally becomes more efficient in how long it takes to move that person through the whole hospital experience, and the degree of an audit trail that's associated with it. Whether it's raw material cracking out of the earth and into the production systems, whether it's the movement of things through those production systems, or whether it's the delivery of service value around those things, it doesn't really matter which part of the economy you point to; once you get to the dictionary and the broker, you get the ability to organize an insanely infinite amount of new business models.

We agree that M2M information brokerage is one of the most significant opportunities in this space. With that, we will be able to achieve a lot more homogeneity of information across multiple platforms.

Today, when we look at, for example, wearable devices, we see a lot of options that are good at any single given task. Some are good for weight management, some for clinical heart-rate monitoring, and some for glucose metering. While on one hand it makes sense, on the other, it's hard to imagine a consumer or a patient willingly wearing multiple devices on their body.

Astro Teller thinks we're heading toward a place where we will have app stores for connected devices in the same way that we have app stores for smartphones. One could download an app for fitness or heart-rate monitoring onto the same unobtrusive body-worn device with the same user experience.

Says Astro:

> Take Match.com, for example. Someone may offer a little widget that shows up in Match.com, then the application will seamlessly use the information from that body monitor via an API that the body monitor provides and will share your mood or type of exercises on Match.com to help you find a better match. It will work the same way that there's an API for the iPhone or the Droid that allowed the same game at a new level of Angry Birds to work on these two very different technology platforms. That means each of the body monitors that want to survive in this world is going to need to have very thoughtfully done application interfaces. They will need to have an equivalent of the APIs and SDKs, the software developer kits that go into the iPad or Samsung Galaxy tablet and all of those things.

According to Astro, similar things are already happening with BodyMedia, Fitbit, and a number of other companies who are already producing SDKs and sharing their APIs. He says:

They may be a little rough around the edges today, but two years from now there's going to be a significant ecosystem, even just two years from today. Basically, now the APIs are there, but the APIs will have to get better. It will take some time for that ecosystem to ramp up. Now that BodyMedia sells hundreds of thousands of armbands a year, it's starting to be plausible to build software applications on top of it. When they were selling tens of thousands a year, it just wasn't worth it. Within a few years we're going to be selling millions of body-worn devices a year. You can imagine a small software company saying, "Okay, let's build an application. We'll pick two or three of these platforms, not fifty, that look like they have the most volume, the best APIs, the best underlying hardware, and we'll bet on some of them." You remember back in the day, there were a lot of different browsers, many of which have fallen away now, but people are mostly just developing on two. A similar thing will happen here.

A quantum leap that will have to happen with the Internet of Things is information sharing among companies, organizations, and device makers. The more open a system, the more innovation will be possible as others discover the value of information and build applications around it.

Glen Allmendinger is a big believer in open systems. He says:

This is a hard subject to make simple, but if you try and make it simple, the thing that you're measuring in any kind of application context is essentially, how free is the data to be used by other peer functions, applications, or businesses or otherwise? Apple and

Google have organized a significant means of creating semiclosed systems. Facebook, in my estimation, is really a closed system that has a huge amount of user-generated content value. If you imagine a future world where you introduce devices into these kinds of systems that allow for content creation by the device or person or both, or the interactions therein, that creates a huge opportunity for open-data sharing.

For example, if you think about just simple, basic problems like repair of equipment in a hospital, you look at the number of people that can touch that piece of equipment [in a way that adds value], and if you made the information around the use of that equipment completely open, you can integrate the people in the hospital who prepared that piece of equipment, the third-party service providers, the actual OEMs, and everybody else who might have a need to touch that piece of equipment when it's used. Then you can create huge compound value even before you forget how to reward everybody for sharing that information.

Of course, things like this are only possible with presumed security and clear, defined rules about who has permission to access the data and under what circumstances. In addition, this vast amount of data will have to be processed and analyzed, and decisions will have to be made based on this data and the data that will be looped back into the whole—the feedback loop—and communicated to either consumers who are using the device, medical professionals, or anybody else.

The company that figures it out might become the first trillion-dollar company. However, a lot needs to happen in terms of regulation and standardization to get there. In the meantime, humans will have to do a lot of strategic thinking and planning, in a not too dissimilar way from the winners of the freestyle chess tournament.

In the next chapter we will look into the key areas of the Internet of Things.

Chapter 4

CORE APPLICATION DOMAINS

*Any sufficiently advanced technology is
indistinguishable from magic.*
~ Arthur C. Clarke

In 1998, when the World Wide Web was on the rise and many companies wondered how it would affect their businesses, Nicholas Negroponte wrote in the foreword to *Unleashing the Killer App:*[20]

> You can see the future best through peripheral vision. Sometimes, looking straight ahead—even with the most dedicated attention and seasoned experience— just misses both the big picture and the new ideas, because they often come at you from those outlying

---

[20] Larry Downes and Chunka Mui, *Unleashing the Killer App: Digital Strategies for Market Dominance* (Boston: Harvard Business Review Press, 1998).

areas affectionately called "left field." Ironically, the more successful you and your company are, the more likely that you'll miss those seemingly orthogonal ideas. Success can be your worst enemy.

The question corporate executives were asking at the time was, "What is your digital strategy?" Today, as we approach the last mile of connectivity with the physical world around us, the question is, "What is your M2M strategy?" M2M is going to affect every company on the same order of magnitude as the Web did in the '90s.

In this chapter we will look at several areas we believe are going to get disrupted and significantly transformed by the Internet of Things and M2M technology. For the sake of discussion, we decided to focus on connected cities, connected homes, connected health, and connected cars.

While we're only scratching the surface in our discussion of these areas, they'll give you a good idea of what's in store with the Internet of Things and, hopefully, inspire you to imagine other innovations that might affect various industries.

CONNECTED CITIES

Cities are an engine of future growth. Specifically, according to McKinsey Global Institute,[21] over the next fifteen years the share of the world's GDP in the top six hundred cities is supposed to double, the share of the world's population living in the cities will keep growing, and the per capita GDP in the cities will grow by over 50 percent. The population in cities is slated to grow from 3.5 billion in 2010 to 6.2 billion in 2050. Cities are

---

[21] McKinsey Global Institute, *Global Cities of the Future: An Interactive Map* (2012). http://www.mckinsey.com/insights/economic_studies/global_cities_of_the_future_an_interactive_map.

becoming bigger and wealthier. This has significant implications
for energy consumption, transportation, and parking, as well
as public safety and overall urban logistics.

Fortunately, thanks to consistently improving Machine-
to-Machine technologies, our cities are becoming smarter,
too. Sensors and real-time wireless communication allow for
better energy management, traffic optimization, and building
automation.

Anthony Flint[22] wrote on the website The Atlantic Cities
that smart cities are not just about helping people find a place
to park; they are also designed to help cities in the developing
world better manage population growth as it affects energy
management, transportation, water supply management, and
sanitation services.

Says Assaf Biderman:

> The city is becoming like a computer in the open
> air. All the networks—telecommunications, trans-
> portation, energy—are getting digitized for better
> management. But at the same time, you can think
> of them as a huge nervous system that tells you a
> lot about what's going on in the city in real time.
> Where are masses of people? How do people con-
> nect? How is information flowing and how are
> resources allocated? Where and how do things move?
> Machine-to-Machine is about objects around you
> telling you what they do and where they are. Now,
> if you give developers open APIs to all this data,
> people can play with it and mash it up: Companies,

---

[22] Anthony Flint is a fellow at the Lincoln Institute of Land Policy, a think
tank in Cambridge, MA. (Source: http://www.theatlanticcities.com/authors/
anthony-flint/.)

individuals, city halls, you name it, can start to build vast knowledge from all this data about cities. You can almost think about it as the Web merging itself with the city. That marriage is very interesting. That is a radically new development. If you go back two decades it was almost unthinkable.

The notion of a city as a giant living organism is not new—it was portrayed, for example, in Fritz Lang's 1927 movie *Metropolis*. However, for the first time in history this notion is becoming a reality by using wireless technology and connected devices and sensors.

Assaf continues:

This is what the MIT SENSEable City Lab is about: a sensible city, a city that senses and responds constantly. Everything in it comes in conversation with something else. It's up to us to design it and to plan it and to manage it. When I say *us*, I mean the academics, the industry, all public employees, but mainly, the citizens. It's a new time when suddenly there's a much broader access to the environment in terms of how it can be managed.

In reality, the promise of capturing and processing information in real time from various sensors around the city—transportation, pollution, waste management, energy, and so on—is very powerful. It has the potential to democratize information and give more power to citizens. And with that democratization and sharing of information and responsibility, a lot of things become possible.

Assaf shares an exciting vision of this potential:

All of a sudden, we're almost going back to old days of ancient Greek democracy with empowered citizens. We now have a capacity to influence, design, make decisions and suggestions about life in the city by learning about how our city and our environment is managed. People can start asking, "What can you do to make it a better place: more efficient, safer, cleaner, etc.? What are the new ways to think about energy management, the removal chain, and pollution?"

If local governments don't necessarily need to focus on execution and operations so much anymore, but more on governing, that is also a different situation. If, instead of having to design the management system for the transport network for each city top down, you crowd-source it or take it from another city with relevant data—have the solution come out from start-ups, individuals, NGOs, corporations, you name it—then the city government takes a new role. It would ensure that minorities get as much service as majorities do, that budgets are allocated correctly, that the experts and planners use their expertise for the public good. There's room for this new citizenship. There's change in government and there's change in the functionality of the city. There's also change in business models. New business models become possible when you start to connect so many things together and put people in between.

We find this vision fascinating. It would allow city inhabitants to simply know what is going on in the city—what the pollution map looks like, where the trash goes, and what is happening with traffic and public transportation. All this information is going to help them become better citizens and manage their own cities better.

Another big aspect of connected cities is energy management. "Everything is changing about energy right now," says John Elliott, managing director of mobility product & offering development at Accenture, and formerly senior director of product management at Qualcomm. He continues:

> It's just fascinating to watch it. For the last thirty or forty years we've been increasingly dependent on offshore for our energy needs. Now we see all of that changing with the fracking technology breakthrough. At the same time, the heavy government investment in sustainability carries with it an implicit benefit for the little guy. Investments in sustainability can enable microgrids. For example, if you generate excess energy on your rooftop solar panel, it can be stored in your neighborhood's energy-dense capacitors and batteries, and then sold to and consumed on demand by the neighbors.

M2M technology is critical for the manifestation of the idea of microgrids, where energy is generated when the sun and wind are available and then locally consumed on demand. Knowing in real time how much energy has been produced, how much excess energy is available, and how much is being consumed are absolutely critical to ensure an uninterrupted flow of electricity.

CONNECTED HOMES

Better energy management leads us into people's homes and to the topic of connected homes. As we discussed, individual homes can become not only energy consumers, but also energy producers by providing for their own energy and potentially selling the excess energy back to the grid. This way, homes are going to become more environment and energy aware. But smart, connected homes are about much more than just efficient energy management; they are also about comfort and convenience for their inhabitants. By better managing the lighting, temperature, smart appliances, security, and entertainment systems, homes are going to be adapting to people.

For example, by sensing whether people are in the house or which rooms they are in, a smart thermostat can either switch off heating or cooling completely or concentrate on the rooms where the people are—both improving the energy consumption and making people more comfortable. Lights can be dimmed automatically, depending on the time of day, who's in the room, and what that person is doing.

Astro Teller takes it a step further and believes people will be able to control things like lighting and temperature by unobtrusive body sensors that would automatically communicate with the home's systems if a person is too hot or too cold. In a room full of people, a smart thermostat could select an average optimal temperature for the group based on their collective body sensor readings.

Says Astro:

> It will be this ubiquitous computing, this machine-to-machine interface, where your body is now radiating via something that's right by your body out to the world. Here's who I am. Here's what I need. Here's what I like. What matters is that it's on your body and that it's sending this information out and that a ton of the things that we do now explicitly will become implicit. In order to make them implicit, you

have to have this Machine-to-Machine conversation going on kind of behind the curtain.

Smart home appliances can ensure we never run out of things like mineral water, juice, or milk by tracking consumption in our household and alerting us before something is completely consumed—similar to the way your car tells you it's about to run out of gas.

John Elliott makes the following predictions about home appliances:

> All major appliances are going to be connected, and the value of the information from major appliances will be worth a lot for those appliance manufacturers. Not only will they discover usage patterns, but also ways to better manage marketing and supply chain around parts replacement by staying connected with their installed base.

We believe that monitoring and gathering information by home appliances for the purpose of better serving the consumer will justify making them connected. It will also open new opportunities to use collected data. John continues:

> Even though the primary use case in the example I gave is an opportunity to syndicate data externally to appliance manufacturers, there will be an interest in this data in the long haul by other parties. Some of the new entrants, like Google, have a very different view of the value of data, and as they wake up to this opportunity you may see them investing more heavily and creating a sort of platform for home appliance data.

We also talked to Panos Nasiopoulos, director of the Institute for Computing, Information, and Cognitive Systems at the University of British Columbia. One of the initiatives of the Institute is creating smart living spaces with reduced environmental impact while improving the life of the occupants. In doing this, the Institute works with various industry and academic players and uses multidisciplinary teams.

We talked about the old connected-home stereotype—soon my fridge is going to talk to my toaster and my coffeemaker will talk to my food processor. At some point there may be a valid reason for this type of connectivity, but Panos' idea is that we often hear strange and unnatural use cases for connected homes just because they seem to be technically feasible. In short, there should be a reason your coffeemaker needs to talk to your food processor. Technologists often forget aspects of human behavior and its adaptability. Ultimately, connectivity is supposed to *improve the quality of life and the standard of living*, just as home appliances did fifty years ago.

According to Panos, non-intrusiveness and immediate value are critical for the adoption of connectivity in the home. For example, if my appliances start telling me how I can use them more effectively to achieve better results and save electricity, I may be prepared to pay more for them. In the longer term, appliances would learn how people live and behave, which would give manufacturers a wealth of information on how to design better appliances. Of course, proper security and privacy mechanisms will need to be in place to ensure that the appliances cannot be hacked into.

Going forward, connected devices at home will measure the productivity of home tasks, and they will measure people's mood by using body sensors. Analysis of all this data in aggregate will afford the opportunity to build a better understanding of how humans live in their homes and what can help them to have better, more comfortable, and more productive lives.

CONNECTED HEALTH

Another important aspect of connected homes is the health of their inhabitants. Especially with the aging population and the growing number of people with chronic diseases like diabetes, monitoring is becoming especially necessary and helpful. In that way, the home can become not only a comfortable living space, but also an environment that helps people stay healthy and can even save lives. This brings us to the topic of connected health.

When we speak of connected health, we mainly see two groups that will be significantly affected by the Internet of Things. The first is hospital and clinical processes. From tracking hospital assets and patients with RTLS and RFID, to replacing bulky wired body sensors with unobtrusive wireless ones, to remotely monitoring hospital equipment, the world of health care is in for some dramatic changes. The other major group to be affected is consumer medical devices: Soon, they will be able to give consumers tools to manage their own health by better understanding their lifestyle and what is happening in their body between doctor visits.

Regarding the latter category, John Major comments:

> I think it's insane to go to your doctor's office to get a blood-pressure reading. A machine should know and should be sending you and your doctor notes if something is out of the ordinary. It should be like your bank notifying you when your checking account is overdrawn. I really visualize every human body connected to the network. That means a lot of worn, nonintrusive biomedical devices. Many

of those devices will be embedded in the clothes you're wearing.

Integrating sensor data that comes from a patient's body or from medical equipment with electronic health records has the tremendous potential of providing a rich context for a person's health. John Elliott said, "When someone checks into an emergency room, they touch twenty-seven different devices, and right now there's no way to make use of that data." Total integration and use of these data sets would enable doctors and caregivers to detect early warning signs in someone's health. For example, it would help determine if a person is not eating, as detected by a refrigerator door that did not open or close for several days.

John also believes in the significant potential of virtual care. He says, "You can send a nurse practitioner into the field with a tablet and have her access a panel of specialists, who can diagnose and treat someone in a very remote location. That's an extraordinary value."

Another significant area where the Internet of Things can make a difference is chronic disease management. Connected devices and sensors can help track patients' adherence to medications, results of drug trials, and follow-ups to initial patient visits. These smart devices can share information with physicians such as glucose-level readings, blood-pressure monitoring, abnormal heart activity, changes in skin color, and so on. Of course, this kind of information and the ease of communicating it presents challenges to the Health Insurance Portability and Accountability Act (HIPAA); there need to be regulations on who can have access to patients' data and under what conditions.

The more devices that collect data in a patient's home, the richer the context will be for understanding the patient's health. Things like weight, metabolism, perspiration, and blood pressure, in aggregate, can tell a better story over time about what is happening with a patient.

We spoke with Dr. Peter Kuhn of the Scripps Research Institute, who believes the power of providing immediate feedback of the patient's condition—the kind of power that is provided by connected devices—is absolutely necessary for further development of proper treatment. He also believes understanding patient context is very important for early cancer detection in a noninvasive way.

Multiple hurdles in health care currently slow down the adoption of connectivity at its most useful opportunity. Says Steve Pazol:

> It takes a long time for connected devices to get FDA-validated, and then it takes a long time to get those devices to the point where they can be reimbursed by insurance. I think that's a big challenge. You have to show that this connected device is going to give better efficacy than what's currently out there. It's just expensive to go through trials to prove that. It's hard to experiment, hard to get insurance companies on board, and the latter are reluctant to pay without guarantees that it saves lives.

Bill Davidson adds:

> I believe emerging markets will be the first places that we see health care and wireless come together. I worry about the [FDA] certification process, but I also worry about the regulatory environment in the developed markets. The lawyers in the developed markets may treat new solutions as a guarantee that the patient won't ever have a heart attack or

that they won't die from one. It isn't a guarantee; it is a way to put more information in the hands of the person who wants to monitor themselves and create more of a consumer electronics model around health care so that patients have more control. The emerging markets might have more of that kind of mentality, so I think it will start there. I think consumers in developed countries will start to see and ask, "Why can somebody in India get service like this and I can't get it here?" Then it will pull through. I actually think the innovation in health care will happen in the emerging markets.

Dr. Peter Kuhn also believes we have not yet found the right model for connected health that would satisfy patients, hospitals, regulatory bodies, and insurance companies. But this should not prevent us from trying to find it.

In reality, consumer health care can save lives. Says Peggy Smedley:

Ford is working with the health care industry on a solution that would notify a nearby hospital if you were having a heart attack in your car, which can send an ambulance before you even know you were having one. We can find medical cures that were never possible before because we can gather information that we were never able to before.

Glenn Lurie of AT&T makes the following observations:

I believe that you'll see some breakthroughs in e-health and e-wellness in the near future. Also automotive, I think, is going to blow up. We're talking about two hundred fifty million cars on the road in the U.S. today, with less than 5 percent of them having a wireless module built in. We see that exploding over the next couple of years.

CONNECTED CARS

Indeed, as Glenn Lurie says, cars are getting smarter as well. Says Bill Davidson:

> Think about the time frame in the early 1990s: Yes, you had computers in cars, but nowhere near as many as we have today. And the generation before that, there were really no computers in cars. Cars were purely mechanical and had no means of communication. Today there are probably forty computers in your car—individual sensors and microprocessors that have the capability to tell you something.

Astro Teller adds:

> There are lots of decisions that are being made by machines in a car. Today you press the brake pedal on your car and something very complex is happening behind that brake pedal. It feels like a mechanical action, but the electronic antilock system is actually running this control system to try to get you the most braking action without skidding.

Many cars have *drive by wire* implemented, whereby the steering wheel is not mechanically connected to the wheels anymore, but controls a motor, which controls the wheels. In addition, modern cars are filled with sensors: detecting light for the mirrors and headlights and rain for the windshield wipers, tire pressure monitors, accelerometers, gyroscopes, and compasses.

Going further down this path, the digitalization of mechanics in cars allows for the arrival of driverless cars or self-driving cars, which Google has successfully tested over the past few years. But connectivity offers even more: communication between cars to optimize traffic flow and make better decisions on behalf of the driver. Volvo, for example, has successfully demonstrated road trains as part of the EU's SARTRE (Safe Road Trains for the Environment) Project, which has several cars following one another in a platoon formation; the lead car has a professional driver taking responsibility for the platoon, while following vehicles operate in a semi-autonomous mode, reducing the distance between the vehicles, and reducing drag and fuel consumption, while getting to their destination faster.[23]

You may be familiar with the crowd-sourced navigation application Waze, which is one of the most accurate personal navigation applications today because it uses real-time traffic and construction information provided by users. For example, it can get you from Palo Alto to San Francisco during rush hour within five minutes of the ETA. But it still requires physical user input. What if we take this concept a notch further and imagine cars automatically populating an application like this with real-time data like speed, acceleration, weather conditions, and more? Without any physical user intervention we would have very accurate maps of traffic, as an example. Cars can also communicate with one another and suggest the optimal speed to the driver to get to his or her destination sooner.

Today, a rapidly growing industry using connected cars is Usage-Based Insurance, or UBI. Led by Progressive, the

---

[23] SARTRE, *Partners Conclude After the SARTRE Project* (2012). http://www .sartre-project.eu/en/about/news/Sidor/20120917_1.aspx.

concept enables insurance companies to manage risk by better understanding driver behavior. Safe driving behavior gets rewarded with lower insurance premiums, which leads to more safe drivers on the roads.

OnStar by GM was one of the first successful connected car applications. Not only does it provide remote assistance, it also has a digital crash signature, based on wide-ranging vehicle sensor data, which notifies emergency services and hospitals of a car crash and potential injuries.[24]

Just as with other industries, data generated by car sensors will have value that goes beyond the use cases of remote diagnostics, road assistance, navigation, UBI, or inter-car communication. Real-time car data can be used to populate the city traffic map, predict participation at events, monitor pollution, and build predictive models for drivers' behavior. This data can potentially be sold or licensed to interested parties. Says John Elliott:

> If you're interested in vehicle speed relative to speed limit, how fast you speed, you slow down, how many right turns, how many left turns you make, things like that, either for driver coaching or Usage-Based Insurance applications or something like that, it would be super helpful to be able to subscribe to just that data, purely that data.

All in all, with Machine-to-Machine connectivity, cars will become their drivers' smart companions to help navigate traffic better, make critical road decisions faster, sense the driver's

---

[24] Economist Intelligence Unit, *Rise of the Machines: Moving from Hype to Reality in the Burgeoning Market for Machine-to-Machine Communication* (2012). http://digitalresearch.eiu.com/m2m/report.

well-being, and entertain drivers while on the road without distracting from the important task of driving.

OTHER POTENTIAL INDUSTRIES

Another ideal candidate for disruption by M2M technology is the supply chain, where real-time visibility and monitoring can have a direct and immediate effect on efficiency and cost savings. According to John Elliott:

> We do believe that M2M in its most basic sense is nothing more than a logical extension of ERP software. It's back to real-time enterprise. So if you've moved to real-time manufacturing, you're probably already doing some of this to a certain extent, maybe just not calling it M2M. I do believe that everything from industrial lighting to supply chain that has an SAP or Oracle module definitely has need for Machine-to-Machine connectivity.

Looking at various industry verticals and their readiness for M2M adoption, Christian Busch makes the following observations:

> Oil, gas, and mining are probably the most advanced because of the nature of the business, specifically things like gas leaks down in the mine. You have worker safety regulations that you need to act on very quickly. Logistics, like load tracking, package tracking, FedEx, DHL, and so on would also benefit greatly. Another industry is equipment leasing and rental—things like construction equipment and power generators on construction sites. They are billed by the hour. You want to make sure that the

generator is working at all times. If it is at risk to
break down, you want to send a service technician
very quickly to exchange it.

We don't yet know what other applications can be developed
using the data from various industries and verticals, but there
is a belief that there will be a market for this data, which will
further boost innovation. John Elliott predicts:

> We see a model where there is a secondary market
> for data, subject to laws and regulations, within each
> jurisdiction. There is a possibility to syndicate analyt-
> ics. The big data engines, like SAP or Microsoft, can
> pull the data off the connected devices and make the
> streams of data available to interested third parties.
> It could be any number of value chain participants,
> and think of it almost like the cable model, where
> others can subscribe to this data.

Says Glen Allmendinger:

> I've always used this notion of simple and complex
> systems. If I'm just connecting an ATM or MRI
> machine onto my own hub-and-spoke remote service
> or remote support system, that's a simple application.
> When there's a ton of confusing data across many
> different types of machines, environments, and
> applications within a hospital, or factory or even a
> city, I call that a complex environment. . . .
>
> When you look at the landscape, the whole world
> out there, you largely still reside within the simple
> environment, with bits and pieces of compound

values starting to eke themselves out naturally. In order to really drive the whole opportunity to a much, much, much broader compound value, obviously there are still a few protocol wars at the device level that need to be sorted out by the connectivity community. But more importantly, this is a move into the whole state-based distributive information architecture that none of the constituents, especially those who grew up in the client-server architecture world, would ever understand how to do.

The big challenges today, according to Glen, are that people don't understand the kind of reference technology architecture that is required to realize the potential of the Internet of Things, and they don't have any idea about the kinds of shared business models. As soon as we fuse data from many different sources, we have to think about how these sources are getting rewarded and how the whole ecosystem is sustaining itself economically.

While there is still a lot of thinking that needs to happen both on the optimized technology architecture side and the business model side, already today we are seeing many successful seeds of the Internet of Things implementation.

Glenn Lurie shares his opinion:

The way you're going to be successful in this space is to look at each vertical separately, because they are separate ecosystems—whether it's health care or automotive, they are all different. The business models have to work for the OEMs, for the carriers, and, most importantly, they have to work for the end users. Those are things, to be honest with you, we are still learning. Those are things that we're still trying. I've got almost sixteen million customers paying me every month on the AT&T network with the emerging devices. We've launched numerous devices and we've learned from business models, whether it's a business model like Amazon where you hide the connectivity or it's a business model like Garmin PND, which includes a certain level of connectivity and then, after, the customer signs up for additional services. We're learning, but I think that each model is going to be independent of that vertical.

It takes an open and unbiased mind to uncover new opportunities and business models, just as Nicholas Negroponte observed at the beginning of this chapter. As we have seen, there is tremendous potential in connected cities, connected homes, connected health, and connected cars, as well as in many other industries. But a lot of learning is happening as we speak and it's not necessarily today's big players who are going to dominate these areas; very possibly it may be companies we don't even know exist today. Solid use cases and a deep understanding of them are required to succeed—and that's what we are going to discuss in the next chapter.

Chapter 5
USE CASES

The use cases capture the goals of the system.
To understand a use case, we tell stories.
~ Ivar Jacobson

In his book *The Innovator's Dilemma*,[25] Clayton Christensen uses a fascinating Harvard Business School case called "Hewlett-Packard: The Flight of the Kittyhawk." The Kittyhawk was the product name of a revolutionary hard disk drive developed by Hewlett-Packard (HP) in the early '90s. The disk was tiny and had a capacity of 20MB to 40MB, which made the product unique at its time with potential to disrupt one or more industries. Yet the sales volume of the disk was disappointing. HP expected to sell seven hundred thousand units over two years, but instead

---

[25] Clayton M. Christensen, *The Innovator's Dilemma: The Revolutionary Book That Will Change the Way You Do Business* (New York: Harper Collins Publishing, 1997).

sold only one hundred sixty thousand, which resulted in the product being cancelled in 1994. What was the problem? Why couldn't such a groundbreaking technology win in the market?

The Kittyhawk team was targeting the emerging market of PDAs (Personal Digital Assistants, the ancestors of modern smartphones, only without Internet connections). To serve that market, the hard drive had to be more robust and withstand a one-meter fall test, which drove the cost up to about double what it could have been without the robustness. The Kittyhawk met these requirements and would have been excellent. However, the PDA market was not ready to take off: It took years to grow into a market large enough to benefit from innovations like the Kittyhawk disk.

In the meantime, Nintendo had its portable game consoles, and more and more games were being sold. The new games were stored on cartridges, which took up a lot of space—especially in a kid's backpack. HP's Kittyhawk would have been an ideal solution for Nintendo, and it did not even need to be super-robust for that (which would have made manufacturing the disk easier). The market for game consoles exploded in the early '90s, but HP completely missed it because they were chasing the wrong target.

The story demonstrates how critical it is to pick the right market and, crucially, the right use case for the technology. Good understanding of use case drives market selection. As we discovered in chapters 1 and 2, many critical technologies are available for M2M. But the question is, what is the right use case that would bring value to customers and drive revenue?

Businesses, especially new businesses, live and die by use cases. A use case defines exactly what a user is going to do with the product or service and why he/she is going to do that. For example, if we describe a use case for tracking assets within a hospital, we would see the following: A nurse is looking for an IV pump, which is urgently needed in the operating room. She pulls out her smartphone, launches an app, types in *IV pump*, and within seconds the app shows her several available IV pumps in her immediate surroundings, ranked by distance. She walks to the nearest one and brings it to the OR.

In total, the solution saves her hours a week looking for IV pumps and other assets, such as portable EKG devices and defibrillators. The solution is priced in such a way that it costs a fraction of the money it saves the hospital. This is a successful use case. The technology that supports this use case consists of an active RFID tag attached to every asset, which communicates its position to access points installed throughout the hospital. The data from the tags is sent over the local network to a server, which overlays the tag position information with the floor plans of the hospital. Finally, the application, which demonstrates where all assets are located, can be accessed from a desktop computer, a laptop, a tablet, or a smartphone.

Usually, it's easier to come up with a use case that solves a well-known (old) problem in a new way (through technology), as just described in the asset-tracking use case. It's much harder to come up with a new use case that solves a lesser-known problem, like what we sometimes find in healthcare. But companies, especially start-ups, do it all the time. Sometimes they win, more often they lose, but in the end, the new use cases are the ones that open tremendous new opportunities for value and growth.

For example, we can make a case that every pair of exercise or running shoes would benefit from being connected to the Internet. Let's look at it: First, many people exercise unevenly, distributing more weight on one leg than the other, which can lead to injuries. Wouldn't it be beneficial if your shoes could warn you about your unhealthy exercise habits, so that you can do something about it and avoid an injury? Second, would a manufacturer of running shoes such as New Balance benefit from knowing how their products are being used and how often, and where most wear and tear occurs, so that they can develop better shoes? Finally, wouldn't it be beneficial to have a GPS tracking device embedded in shoes so that a missing person can be easily found?

On the technical side, what's the best way to power such shoes without requiring the user to plug them in regularly or replace batteries? And here's where we come to a major use-case dilemma: If a user does not directly benefit from the connected shoe on a daily basis, he or she will not be bothered with charging or replacing batteries. One way to make something like this work would be to include energy harvesting, for example, converting the kinetic energy of the runner into electricity to power the connectivity modem embedded in the shoe. The best use cases are those where the end user does not need to do anything to ensure uninterrupted service.

Just a few years ago, most use cases associated with M2M were focused on monitoring industrial assets. In the article "Four Strategies for the Age of Smart Services," Glen Allmendinger writes, "For customers, smart services create an entirely new kind of value—the value of removing unpleasant surprises from their lives."[26] Indeed, with hard data provided by sensors and connected devices, we know; without it, we just guess and estimate. That happens with usage-based insurance, for example. While knowing versus guessing is still at the core of most M2M use cases, the understanding has evolved to include a much broader context—the ability to not only collect information, but to also do something about it on the spot, dynamically, such as remotely changing pricing on vending machines or providing immediate customer feedback.

---

[26] Glen Allmendinger and Ralph Lombreglia, "Four Strategies for the Age of Smart Services," *p.2*

Says Christian Busch of SAP:

> To give you an example, let's say a beverage company wants to optimize the assortment in their vending machines. They have a machine in a hospital and a machine in an office. They want to make sure that each machine makes maximum profit, so they need different products. They have forty thousand machines. To optimize this manually is impossible. You need an algorithm that takes in all the transactional data, looks at what is being sold and to whom, the location, how many people work there, and so on—all in real time. The next time the truck gets loaded, it gets loaded with the right product and the right quantities.
>
> We think vending is close to being disrupted by M2M because most vending-machine companies currently operate manually. In our case, we saw that optimizing the distribution to vending machines based on real-time data results in double-digit revenue increase. In addition, they are able to adjust prices based on demand and to run promotions on those machines. This is new in the vending-machine industry because changing the price of a product dynamically in a vending machine is unheard of so far. It will take them to a new level of efficiency in their operations. I think that's a perfect example of the power of M2M.

Mark Wells shares his experience of successful and unsuccessful use cases and the power of direct user feedback:

> We started with tracking teen drivers. The statistics for teenage drivers are horrible—one in twenty kids

is either disabled or killed within three or four years of getting their driver's license. You would think you'd do everything you could to stop it from happening to you. And yet there wasn't a big market of parents willing to put a tracking device on their kid's car to monitor unsafe driving. It's the strangest thing, we thought. . . .

On the other hand, a company called DriveCam had an idea to put little cameras in shuttle buses and other commercial vehicles. The camera was pointed at the driver, so the driver could see it, and it had a little red light on it. If the driver did anything that was considered unsafe, such as hard braking, rapid acceleration, sharp cornering as measured by an accelerometer on the camera, the little light would come on and the camera would record a video for ten seconds back and ten seconds forward. Later your boss could review it to see why that happened and if it led to any accidents.

The interesting thing was that within a day of installing that camera, it became a game among the drivers to prevent that light from coming on, because nobody wanted to be considered a bad driver. And unless there was an accident there was no video; people became conscious of that. DriveCam wanted to get the same service going with teen drivers, and they finally got it with American Family. While they've had some success, it was also a struggle and has not taken off the way that they had hoped, compared to the commercial market, where it has grown into a big business.

While it's hard to tell exactly why the use case with commercial vehicles has been much more successful than the one with teen drivers, it seems to be an overall trend in M2M so far that B2B use cases have been getting more traction than most consumer cases. Part of the reason may be that the consumer markets are not driven as much by ROI as the enterprise markets are, plus consumer markets require a lot more tweaking with user experience and pricing.

Another critical point from Mark Wells' example is the importance of direct user feedback. One of the areas where it makes a big difference is consumer health care.

As we discussed in the previous chapter, consumerization of health care is a big trend that helps us stay fit and healthy between doctor visits. This trend opens up a whole range of use cases and opportunities. We spoke with Ivo Stivoric, CTO of BodyMedia, a company that makes "dashboards for the human body," as he described them, or portable wearable devices. Says Ivo, "In order to have dashboards for the human body, you have to measure the body, analyze those measurements, and present it back to people in the way that makes sense. Feedback is important. It could be used for a lot of different things."

BodyMedia focuses primarily on weight management today. According to the latest census, over 60 percent of people in the United States are overweight, a third of whom are actually obese. The latter category has a lot of health risks associated with it. As a result, 21 percent of all health care costs in the United States are obesity related, and the numbers are increasing.

Says Ivo:

> People need tools to measure their condition, because you can't manage what you can't measure. We're clueless as to how much we really burn, how much we really eat, how our lifestyles are

affecting these conditions. If you could track your blood-sugar level or monitor your sleep patterns over time and see them getting better because of your lifestyle changes, you can start looking at the world a little differently.

When BodyMedia started twelve years ago, there weren't any wearable monitoring products. Most monitoring devices were either for performance athletes or for clinically sick people. There was nothing in the middle for those who just wanted to be fit and healthy. Ivo continues:

> We built hardware, software, and Web applications accessible from any Internet device. We had to build all these tools ourselves. We worked hard on creating a user interface that was easy to understand without overwhelming people with data. Our device has five body sensors: a three-axis accelerometer to detect movement, activity, and orientation; skin temperature; body heat flux; galvanic skin conductivity response; and near-body ambience. We're adding an ECG sensor to the system. We figured out a way to simplify it so that someone can just slide the armband on and it works. We continue to look at new sensors as new opportunities.

BodyMedia was able to develop sophisticated algorithms to measure a person's physical activity and energy expenditure. As Ivo says:

> From the multi-sensors we can tell if you are sitting or walking, or running, or biking, or weight lifting, and then we can apply the right algorithm

that's personalized for you with your own sensor values. Certain lifestyle activities affect people differently. We had people with diabetes and sleep apnea coming to us. Diabetes in particular is a very personalized condition. Everyone's metabolic system handles it differently. So wouldn't it be nice to know how your lifestyle is affecting your glucose levels? If you change your lifestyle, then maybe you have a chance to adjust your glucose level just with those changes alone. Maybe even get off medication. The same thing is true for sleep apnea, COPD, or cardio diseases. Everyone knows they need to move more and eat better, but that doesn't necessarily always happen without direct feedback.

BodyMedia users' addiction to data about themselves is what drove Ivo to make his device wireless, connecting to a phone over Bluetooth, and also offering direct wide-area, always-on, real-time connectivity on the device going forward.

Again, Ivo states:

Without real-time connectivity we couldn't put a log in. We couldn't see trends. Once we made our device talk to a phone over Bluetooth, there was a nice way to have your decisions in your hand. You saw your calorie balance for the day. You could also see before going to bed at night that you haven't been sleeping for real the last few days. You thought you lay down for eight hours, but you actually got only four hours of sleep. Now you could decide to go to bed early to catch up on your sleep, because it's just going to continue to affect you. The feedback on the connected device was great.

As the M2M awareness started picking up, some people started asking Ivo and his team, "Why don't you guys connect this thing for real?" The idea was that having real-time sensor information in the cloud, bypassing the phone, would allow other people—caregivers or just loved ones, for example—to have access to it, or the system could just be monitoring a person automatically in real time. Also, having the device connect directly to the Internet simplifies potential user interaction. Adds Ivo:

> As you know, grandmothers don't really understand how to pair Bluetooth devices. Even with Bluetooth LE coming out, it's still a manual process. With a wireless embedded modem, an armband just chirps every hour to the cloud and the data shows up. All Grandma would have to do is slide the device on, it turns on, and it's connected.

In addition to their device, Ivo and his team came up with a disposable adhesive patch with embedded sensors, which could be used for seven days. Ivo says:

> The reason we actually developed the patch is to give people a taste of BodyMedia without having to invest a whole year or six months. We found some corporate wellness partners very interested in the patch, because today their risk assessments are pencil and paper and very subjective. The patch changes that. When they say they work out three times a week, do they really? When they say they sleep okay, do they really?

We talked to Ivo about consumerization of health care and the way real-time data can play a role in preventive medicine. According to Ivo:

> A computer can now look at your data and start finding specific patterns that a human or a doctor can't. When we go for a physical every year, we have momentary snapshots—we don't have real-time data today. Nobody knows what happens in between doctor visits. I think the real-time data is what's missing today when people talk about big data like health care records and so forth. But the technology is there to provide it.

> But in the end, it's the data analytics that is going to drive the value of the real-time data. Just because I have this device on my arm, no one is going to wear it if it doesn't tell me anything useful. Also, no doctor wants to see the conductivity of your skin thirty-two times a second for the last two years. It means nothing to them. You have to simplify the data in terms that will make sense to people, and different applications require different pieces. We intend to play a role in analyzing and simplifying big data. We don't have to build all the apps; other people have our APIs and have started to build apps.

Going forward, Ivo envisions multiple devices, such as glucometers or scales or even thermostats and lighting in the house, talking to his device. "You put all these things together," he says, "and you start to have a very rich context of understanding.

I think it's more of the promise of big data that you can start to do really important health care things."

There is a whole range of new use cases being tested. One impressive example is Muse, a device by Canadian start-up InteraXon. Muse goes on a person's forehead, holding itself like glasses behind the person's ears, and measures brainwaves. It sends the brainwave data to a mobile phone or a large-screen TV, and the person can play games using his or her mind. For example, users can initiate a virtual snowfall in a village or cause a solar eclipse by increasing their concentration level. We see a huge potential in this direct feedback application for helping people be more present, focused, and mindful—all crucial for personal productivity.

We have also seen a company that puts wireless sensors in the soil, which measures the moisture in the soil and the amount of salinity. As a result, farmers, golf course groundskeepers, wine growers, and others can save significant amounts of water and money, while ensuring at the same time that grass and plants receive the necessary amounts of moisture.

We also spoke with Assaf Biderman about the project MIT SENSEable City Lab did in Copenhagen, called Copenhagen Wheel. Assaf describes his product as a little connected wheel that attaches to the rear wheel of a bicycle. He says:

> It can go on any rim of any bike. It's totally wireless—everything you need is inside one unit: battery, modem, controller, electric motor, power generator, sensors, microprocessors, and a Bluetooth transceiver. You can basically twist two screws, put it on your bike, put the chain on, and you're done. Then you download an app on your smartphone, wirelessly connect to the wheel, and activate it. The app on the phone allows you to control the wheel.

For example, you can tell it how much power to multiply your own effort by and the motor will kick in. If you tell it to go twice as strong as you are pedaling, it measures your output and then it basically imitates your pedaling cycles. You don't really feel that there's a motor helping; you just feel like you're stronger.

Assaf explains the use case of his project:

Most modern cities have been built around the automobile in terms of scale, density, and distances. The city topography is often challenging for non-motorized vehicles. With this bike you can make hills seem flat and distances seem short. That's the main goal—let's get more people on bikes, let's get the suburbs on bikes.

Using M2M connectivity enabled Assaf and his team to uncover a whole new value from the device. Again, Assaf explains:

We were also giving people feedback on their phone about distances they traveled and surrounding data. We also embedded air-quality sensors that measure CO, NO_2, relative humidity, and temperature. All the data is collected by the sensors on the wheel and is channeled through the phone to the cloud. With open APIs, anybody can write apps to the wheel. In Copenhagen, as people ride around, each bike populates its own part of a real-time map. You get this very nice crowd-sourced and crowd-sensed map of real-time weather, pollution, and so on.

Steve Hudson of Omnilink started his journey into the world of personal tracking devices in 2004 with a location-based platform to monitor and manage criminals who are assigned to an alternative program instead of being incarcerated. It's well known that jails are overcrowded, but there is also a higher probability of re-offending after jail time, and the costs of keeping people in jail are too high. With a partner, Omnilink developed a wireless device—a rugged and waterproof ankle bracelet—that is impossible to remove without initiating an immediate alert to the parole officer. Omnilink also developed software that enables offenders to be tracked on a map, along with a set of configurable rules. The parole officer can configure the perimeter of where the offender needs to be at different times of the day. The device tracks offenders in real time and provides data to Omnilink's monitoring center, from where it sends alerts to the parole officer if the offender is not complying with his or her location rules.

Says Steve:

> We incorporated some very unique technology that allows us to not only monitor the offender, but through an opt-in process also alert the victim or the judge if the offender is nearby. In a domestic violence case, for example, we offer the victim an opportunity to be alerted on their cell phone if the offender comes within a certain distance of the victim. While we don't share the actual location of the offender with either the judge or the victim, we send them alerts just to be aware.

From there, Steve started looking at additional businesses and verticals they could go into. "We looked and found lots of places where we could track and monitor valuables and provide useful information to manage theft prevention, resource optimization, or simply compliance with responsibilities or regulation," he said. After meeting with the National Alzheimer's Association, Omnilink decided to develop a device and provide a service to Alzheimer's patients and their caregivers. Steve continues:

> The solution is Web-based software that's simplified, but can have a lot of the very complex technology and features that we had in our enterprise application. The problem is that about 50 to 60 percent of Alzheimer's sufferers wander every year, and if they don't return within twenty-four hours, at least half of them will either die or suffer serious injuries. The need for monitoring is very prevalent, especially considering that one out of every two people over the age of eighty-five is getting Alzheimer's. This problem is growing and there is no cure yet. There are billions of dollars in unpaid care with seniors who need to be monitored. None of the existing solutions is perfect today and there isn't a product we can offer that can stay on somebody's arm for more than, let's say, a few days that is reliable enough to track indoors and outdoors. But the technology is advancing.

> We need to give caregivers the ability to see changes in the behavior of their loved ones during the day and night. You typically wouldn't expect your loved one to walk at 2 a.m., but at 2 p.m. Why not? They go on walks, they go to the doctor's, and they even go to work. We want to give them an opportunity to live a normal life as much as possible, which is really

what we're learning to do through this experience of putting [the product] out in the market.

Speaking of monitoring, Sanjay Sarma connected his home to the cloud using X10 surveillance technology and a home networking system from Insteon. As a result, he can control his lights, thermostat, and many other appliances from his phone. Says Sanjay:

> When we travel, my wife is concerned that our cats are okay, so the motion sensors can tell us where the cats have been, which rooms they've been in. Our heating is extremely dynamic; it's motion triggered now instead of being totally time controlled. So the result is that my home is adapting to reality and also controllable from anywhere.

From basic and straightforward use cases, companies go into collecting and overlaying even more data. Bill Davidson recalls a conversation with an executive at San Diego Gas and Electric who said he wanted to use wireless technology to track the weather. Bill asked the executive why he wanted to track the weather, and the executive said:

> Well, we want to connect wireless technology so that when you look at the desert here in San Diego, our peak demand on our electric grid is going to be when we have Santa Ana winds [strong, extremely dry offshore winds]. When the wind comes through the desert, we have absolutely not a cloud in the sky. I want to be able to use solar and I want to be able to use wind. But then when I do not have the Santa Ana, I really would love to be able to track

clouds and know if I need to angle the solar panels southeast instead of northwest to catch maximum sun. The only way I am going to be able to do that is through wireless.

So his thinking is to forget just reading meters; by removing the human cost, which would be the initial cost justification, he is coming up with ways to make the grid more efficient by incorporating wireless technology.

While there seems to be an almost unlimited number of use cases for M2M in various industries and in health care, what about other parts of our lives? For example, how about M2M or connectivity in remote places in Latin America or Africa? We spoke with Bill Toone, president of the ECOLIFE Foundation, who has been actively promoting the conservation of nature around the world.

Bill has led and participated in multiple conservation programs throughout his life, such as the California Condor Recovery Program and other programs like it, which helped restore wild bird populations. Bill makes some very important points about conservation. According to Bill, "In reality, conservation is—and people just don't know it yet—more about saving ourselves. If we don't start taking better care of the resources, the real endangered species will be us." The ECOLIFE Foundation is committed to making a difference, and one way to do it is through technology. "Conservation married with technology is how you change your bottom line," he says.

Bill told us about a use case of putting GPS, heat, and CO_2 sensors into the charcoal ovens that indigenous people in some remote areas in Mexico use to cook their food. The ECOLIFE Foundation puts money into construction of the ovens and then monitors them over time to find out if those stoves really made a difference in the lives of these people and if they are safe.

Specifically, the ECOLIFE Foundation plans to use the real-time connectivity to find out how often the stoves are used and how they are affecting people's health—if there are, for example, dangerous amounts of CO_2 gas. By using GPS coordinates, it's very easy to locate those stoves. We thought it was a great example of using high technology in a low-tech environment, and it's a great potential for M2M.

The more data that is collected by M2M, the more it brings up the question of various use cases and who would benefit most. Glen Allmendinger talks about the primary, secondary, and tertiary uses of data:

> For anything that you connect, there is some primary value. If I think of the connected electric plug example, I can turn the power on and off remotely to anything I connect to it, right? But there's a secondary value that comes from the electric current signature. In the washing machine, the secondary value comes from that smart device's ability to read the current signature and tell if there is some variability in the pattern, which may be traced to the rotor and the motor needing repair. This leads to the third point: The tertiary value was brought to our attention by both Whirlpool and Indesit, an Italian appliance maker. They pointed out that only 50 percent of all people choose the same brand when shopping for the new version of a home appliance. These appliance makers were after usage value. They wanted to know what people did with these machines so they could design them better to meet those needs and essentially create more customer brand loyalty. . . .

Once any device is connected for the primary reason, secondary and tertiary sets of values will flow from there. For example, in the medical equipment space, Steris owns 80 percent of the sterilizers in the health care industry. A sterilizer by itself doesn't have much value. Hospitals buy more sterilization capacity than they really need, so making a case to remotely monitor a sterilizer is essentially dubious. But when you actually look at it as a key chokepoint in the movement of things that conduct surgery, which of course is the most profitable part of a hospital chain economically, then all of a sudden you discover one of these secondary or tertiary values. If I know where the instruments are in the cleaning chain of the supply chain, I know something valuable about my surgery value chain, about the execution and delivery chain. . . .

In all these instances, even before you get the shared data value or data fusion value, people don't realize that once the data is made available, there are lots of things you can do with it in addition to its primary purpose. All of this ties back to this notion of simple, compound, and complex values. For example, like it was done in Dubai with monitoring all the life safety equipment, it was the location app that tied all the emergency vehicles in Dubai to this life safety system. The application allowed them to know if an alarm goes off, where all the available emergency equipment is that might relate to whatever fault that alarm is indicating is in process. In a case of fire, they can quickly deliver a fire truck. While that's a simple version of "compound value," once the data is actually made free to be used by third parties and by adjacent kinds of applications, that's when all of this compounding starts to come into significant play.

As we have seen, there are many recurring themes in successful use cases in M2M: direct user feedback, like in the examples from DriveCam and BodyMedia; feedback plus context, like with BodyMedia, Omnilink, and Copenhagen Wheel; and better risk management, whether for Usage-Based Insurance or tracking valuable assets to prevent theft.

One big challenge in M2M use cases is the disconnection between vertical use cases and horizontal technology platforms. The more each use case is tailored to its customers in terms of device form factors and user experience, the more successful it's going to be. On the other hand, this very tailoring drives up costs and complexity. Finding the right compromise between too much tailoring and using existing horizontal technology platforms is the key in driving the scale of M2M.

Ioannis Fikouras of Ericsson describes this problem this way:

I think the challenge in Machine-to-Machine lies really in solving the commercial problem behind the low-value use cases. And the whole Machine-to-Machine will really fly when we are at the point where we can make these use cases commercially viable. A lot of use cases that people discuss today are actually the high-value use cases. They're high-margin, high-value examples, like expensive medical equipment, security, and related use cases. When people see the life-or-death benefit, they are prepared to pay a lot of money because they have a perceived big advantage when using the service. But if you look at the breakdown of these use cases, they are a very small percentage of the total, maybe just 5 percent.

What I find more interesting are the 95 percent of use cases, which are typically not the sexiest ones and not so life-and-death oriented. These are things like vending machines, or medical cabinets, or connected shopping carts in the supermarket, or some kind of scenario where you have a very low value but incredibly high volumes. From Ericsson's point of view, it's very interesting to think of what are the use cases that maybe are not so attractive per device, but really drive volumes to an order of magnitude higher than these high-margin cases.

In this chapter we looked at some successful and some not-so-successful use cases. Besides giving us an idea of what is possible and what has been working and what has not, reviewing use cases shows us how critical it is to develop a good understanding of a use case or use cases in the M2M area you are pursuing. In the end, as we have seen in the Hewlett-Packard Kittyhawk example, understanding the right use case for the technology leads to choosing a path to successful growth.

Once you understand the use cases and are able to make decisions based on what the market needs and how those needs can be filled, what happens next? In the next chapter we will take a closer look at what is required to take an M2M product to market.

Chapter 6

GETTING TO MARKET

Good judgment comes from experience, but
experience comes from bad judgment.
~ Bruce Dunlevie

One of our favorite Monty Python sketches is the one about the Kilimanjaro expedition. In it, Arthur Wilson (aka Bob), played by Eric Idle, is a young mountaineer who visits the office of Sir George Head, played by John Cleese. During their conversation, it turns out that not only does Sir George Head have a bad case of double vision, he barely understands the complexity of a Kilimanjaro expedition:[27]

Wilson: And what routes will you both be taking?

Head: Good questions . . . shall I? Well, we'll be leaving on January 22nd and taking the following routes. [Goes over to

---

[27] Luke Dempsey, "Monty Python's Flying Circus: Complete and Annotated . . . All the Bits," Python Productions, Ltd., 159. (Source: http://en.wikipedia.org/wiki/Kilimanjaro_Expedition.)

large map, clearly labeled Surrey.] The A23s through Purleys down on the main roads near Purbrights avoiding Leatherheads and then taking the A231s entering Rottingdeans from the north. From Rottingdeans we go through Africa to Nairobis. We take the south road out of Nairobis for about twelve miles and then ask.

Wilson: Does anyone speak Swahili, sir?

Head: Oh, yes, I think most of them do down there. . . ."

In typical Monty Python fashion, an important point is made about how often a lot of attention is paid to nonessential things—specific roads in England—while little attention is paid to the most important parts of the expedition: how to get to Kilimanjaro and whether anybody on the team understands the local language.

A similar thing often happens with the journey to market in M2M. People either focus too much on technology and not enough on other aspects, like user experience, business model, or channel, or they bring in the wrong team that does not speak technical Swahili.

Perhaps at some point it will be possible for non-tech companies that are willing to launch M2M services, such as banks, insurance companies, car manufacturers, retailers, and logistics carriers, to just go about doing their business, using the power and benefits of the Internet of Things without worrying too much about M2M technology, system integration, and so on. The technology will just be there and will supposedly work seamlessly. The success and growth of the Internet of Things will be assured when this time comes.

However, today, getting to market requires paying specific attention to all aspects of the process: from technology to market awareness, ecosystem to business models.

In his book *The Design of Everyday Things*,[28] Donald A. Norman talks about how ease of use of technology helps bring products to market and is ultimately responsible for a product's success. We would like to take a broader view of the phrase *ease of use* and think of it not just in terms of how easy it is to use the final product—how intuitive the user interface is—but also how easy or difficult it is to bring a product to market. A company willing to launch an M2M product is also a user of technology to get this product to market. We will talk about the technology, process, and general business aspects of delivering a product to market in this chapter, and specifically about the business model aspects in the following chapter.

Despite the fact that the technology is readily available for the most part, and prices continue to drop, bringing an M2M product to market is still a complex undertaking. Companies and entrepreneurs have to go through a lot of trial and error before succeeding, and the odds are currently stacked against them.

Often, companies don't realize the level of complexity they're getting themselves into. John Elliott believes executives and engineers consistently underestimate the complexity and the difficulty of getting M2M products to market. As we have seen in previous chapters, the adoption of M2M technologies is moving from traditional tech companies to companies that have little to do with cellular technology.

To realize the potential of the Internet of Things, companies still need to take a deep dive into technology and make sure they have the right talent, or partner with the most competent

---

[28] Donald A. Norman, *The Design of Everyday Things* (New York: Basic Books, 1988).

players, because there are too many things that potentially can go wrong.

Several years ago, I (Daniel Obodovski) was in charge of getting a dedicated location-tracking platform to market. In a nutshell, we provided a chip and reference design, which was meant to enable other companies to build small, low-cost tracking devices with very long battery lives. The platform used GPS signals and a cellular network to determine the location of the device, both outdoors and indoors.

The concept originated from the Qualcomm Research and Development group, which provided several key pieces of technology innovation. First, the reference design was small and enabled creation of very portable devices—about the size of a thumb drive. Most other GPS tracking devices at the time were the size of a brick. Second, it was relatively inexpensive compared to most available devices. Third, it had an intelligent algorithm, which allowed a dramatic extension of battery power up to several months on a single charge. Finally, as mentioned, the device had the capability of providing its location both outdoors and indoors, which most GPS devices could not do at the time.

Who would use such a device and why? From the beginning, we saw huge potential. People could track their loved ones: children, pets, and elderly relatives. Companies could track cargo and packages, law enforcement officers could recover stolen goods, airlines could track lost luggage, and more. The potential could mean millions or tens of millions devices sold.

But before you start selling millions of devices, you have to sell the first one, and you need to know who is going to buy it, why they are going to buy it, and what it is they are actually going to buy. In other words, even though our company only provided the reference design and control server, to ensure the end-to-end success of the product, we had to build the complete ecosystem.

The product's ecosystem included a hardware manufacturer who would build devices based on our reference design, and a distributor who would handle the inventory and take care of order fulfillment, returns, and so on. It also consisted of a wireless carrier who provided the data connectivity to the device and whose network the service was using. It included several Application Service Providers (ASPs) who offered applications for specific markets—in essence, access from a computer or phone to maps where one could see the location of the devices and their activity. Finally, and most importantly, there had to be customers willing to buy the devices and services to fulfill their needs. All of these partners had to be brought together to deliver the end-to-end product.

When I took on that project, my boss warned me that it would be like herding cats, and he was right. The first part of the complexity was managing all these various partners, but without them there was no way of delivering the final product.

Things started moving a lot faster once we found an anchor customer. The anchor customer was one of the top U.S. wireless carriers, who had a large enterprise sales force and saw a need for a low-cost tracking device with long battery life for its customers. It was much easier to line up the distributor and ASPs once we had a customer.

But more challenges were on the way. The device OEM we started working with did not have a lot of experience with enterprise-grade devices, which generally need to be a lot more robust than consumer devices. The OEM kept delaying execution and one day announced bankruptcy. Moving a hardware design to another company proved to be a major undertaking, but after multiple negotiations we succeeded at picking a major OEM who did a fantastic job.

Finally, we figured out hardware issues, overcame the organizational challenges with the wireless carrier, aligned business models of several ASPs, and ended up launching our product in a couple of markets, both consumer and enterprise. Specifically, we launched an enterprise device to track and monitor valuable cargo, a child-tracking device with a major retailer, and an Alzheimer's patient tracking device.

It was time to scale and grow. Our boss, a senior vice president, asked us to come up with what he called a *cookbook*—a simple way for our partners to launch new devices into the market. After several attempts, we realized all of the complexity of launching new devices and services could not be described in a simple cookbook.

John Elliott recalls:

> To this date, how can you explain to a client the *simple* ninety-nine-step process right here? Select a chip and select a module manufacturer and the device design, and then you can upgrade your device, and here's how you certify it with the FCC, and here's how you certify it with an operator. Each of the steps has multiple variables and decision points, and that's just the device sourcing part. Next comes the integration with the carrier's network and application integration. No matter how we tried, we couldn't come up with a simple cookbook. We could tell the cookbook [concept] wasn't enough then; the cookbook [concept] is not enough now.

Complexity kills. However, many things have become simpler, for example, providing connected devices on wireless carrier networks, thanks to CDPs by companies like nPhase, Jasper, and Kore Telematics. Wireless carriers also recognized the need to help their customers get their product to market. Glenn Lurie says of companies launching connected devices, "If they do it better up front, it's cheaper for me as well. It's not just certification. You had to start talking about activation and customer care, you've got to talk about monitoring the device; there are so many aspects that we're going into for many of these players."

Yet getting the hardware right is still a challenge. The market is full of technology players—those who can develop and build a great device, those who can help certify it, those who can write the software, those who can help provide it on the cellular network, those who can integrate it with the back-office software. Yet there is almost nobody who can take you, as a customer, by the hand and walk you through the whole process of bringing a complete M2M solution to market, end-to-end.

Part of the problem is the high fragmentation of M2M markets. According to Dermot O'Shea, CEO and founder of Taoglas, the initial consolidation among M2M hardware manufacturers started in the telematics and UBI space, where devices are becoming more standardized. For example, small, connected devices that plug into the OBD II port of cars are becoming more similar and there are two or three major OEMs building them. Consolidation leads to larger volumes per player, which in turn leads to lower cost and ease of deployment. Outside of telematics and, possibly, electric meters, there's not a lot of high-volume M2M projects out there yet.

Most projects are about five thousand, ten thousand, or perhaps fifty thousand devices, and it's unclear which one will reach hundreds of thousands or millions of units, and when. The paradox here is that because a lot of market experimentation is taking place, one solution does not fit all and it is difficult to aggregate these volumes. As a result, large service-provider companies are reluctant to do a lot of small one-off projects. The companies willing to launch M2M projects are pretty much on their own. Either they have to hire a very experienced and highly technical project manager, who would in turn bring on board all the right companies and contractors to help get the solution to market, or they try to grow the competence in-house by hiring an experienced hardware design team.

The situation is somewhat similar to website development in the mid-1990s with the proliferation of the Internet. Not a lot of people at the time knew where the Internet was going and that it was poised to truly revolutionize the way they did business—and this is the way many view connected devices today. Most businesses recognized that they needed a Web presence—if nothing else, to provide information to their customers and thus cut call-center costs. Companies had a choice of hiring a Web development company or growing the competence in-house within their IT departments. The thing that was fundamentally different, though, was the hardware. By that time there was a significant base of personal computers running Microsoft Windows, thus the hardware risk was minimal.

Not so in the current situation with Machine-to-Machine. The connected devices need to be designed, developed, tested, certified, manufactured, and so on. As a result, hardware is the biggest bottleneck within the M2M landscape.

In addition, wireless technology has both huge advantages and huge challenges. It eliminates wires and makes the location of connected devices a nonissue. At the same time, the position of antennae becomes a critical problem as devices get smaller and more wireless technologies are packed into one device: cellular 2G, 3G, 4G, Wi-Fi, Bluetooth, NFC, and GPS, to name a few.

According to Dermot O'Shea:

> The biggest challenge is that customers don't have experience with cellular wireless. You can buy a precertified module, but you cannot do the same

with an antenna. And the antenna is one of the most common points of failure. Most customers understand software or hardware, but very few have radio frequency or antenna expertise.

We believe and predict that eventually a new type of virtual OEM for M2M will emerge that will be able to bring devices to market fast, while reusing a lot of components and thus minimizing hardware risk. These OEMs will find a way to dramatically simplify the to-market process for hardware and launch new types of devices in small volumes without incurring significant costs. They will be able to quickly iterate and integrate third-party sensors and provision devices on the network with third-party applications.

Already today, wireless modules—boards with all necessary electronic components with the exception of battery, antenna, buttons, LEDs, and cover—have become reusable components. Various modules from the same OEM often have pin-to-pin compatibility, which means it's easy to replace one module with another if different functionality is required. For example, one module can have cellular 3G connectivity only, while another one might have an accelerometer and a couple of sensors on the board as well.

A lot of innovation is happening in the antenna space, too. According to Dermot O'Shea, active antennas—the ones that can self-tune—are already coming to market as part of smartphones. It's possible that for devices of a certain size, antennas will become standardized, thus removing this major point of contention. However, the smaller the device, the more challenging antenna design is going to remain. For example, in the medical space a lot of customization is still required.

Generally, with a few exceptions, it does not make sense for companies launching M2M services to make the devices themselves. In a lot of cases, existing OEMs can make the devices faster and cheaper, as long as they view the business as attractive enough even with low volumes.

In spite of all the complexity and hurdles of bringing new products to market, it's refreshing to see how some companies, by using a nontraditional approach to hardware and rapid iteration, can achieve astounding success. In an M2M best-kept secret, Mark Wells, CTO and founder of Procon, built his company from a trailer in San Diego into one of the key players in the telematics space, ending up with millions of devices sold and a huge private equity deal.

In 2003, Mark, a former Nokia executive and entrepreneur, was mentoring five different companies and watching for the best one so that he could invest in it and run it. One idea that captured Mark's attention was to use used cell phones to track vehicles and monitor teenage drivers. At the time, the used cell phones cost about $5 to $10 each, while brand-new cellular modems cost over $100. That gave Mark's company, Procon, which was called DriveOK at the time, an advantage in the price-sensitive market. Also, by using off-the-shelf used cell phones, Mark did not have to worry about antenna design, carrier certification, or convincing a manufacturer to build low volumes of product for him.

Says Mark:

> We decided to have full control over our destiny—
> build the hardware from old cell phones, have the
> infrastructure, have the relationships with the car-
> riers, and put up a business-to-consumer website,
> literally selling to the parents of teenage drivers
> directly on the Web. The idea was to start selling
> quickly.

Mark set up a website and a tracking application, which enabled its customers to see on Google maps where all the phones were in real time. The application had features like geofence and speed alert, and could indicate whether teenagers were speeding or driving unsafely in any way. For marketing, Procon used Google AdWords, which was brand new at the time and not a lot of people knew about it.

Procon replicated a typical garage start-up. Mark says:

> We had a little eight-hundred-square-foot trailer in Pacific Beach in San Diego, which was our office. No air-conditioning and no heat. In the summertime everyone was in shorts, and sometimes in the winter we would wear gloves. The racks from Costco made up our manufacturing line.

Procon built their first hardware by tearing apart used cell phones they bought from T-Mobile and using the internal circuit board for communication. T-Mobile had an excess of used cell phones, which they got from people trading in their old phones for new ones. They gladly sold those used phones at bargain-basement prices. Mark and his team just removed the covers, screens, and keyboards, attached a GPS board, battery, and power cable, and put it in a new housing. All devices were then tested and shipped to the customers.

Mark recalls:

> We weren't the first ones who thought about tracking cars and fleets with GPS, but we had this huge cost advantage. Also, we were the ones who turned it into a non-enterprise-level sale: Just buy off the Web and we would ship devices to your place. The

great thing about our business was that the revenue was coming from hardware plus the monthly subscription. We made a little bit of money on the hardware and learned quickly to sell a yearly service plan bundled with the hardware. We offered a 20 to 30 percent discount for the bundle and in return got all the money up front. That model ended up supporting our whole venture, because we were getting all the cash from subscriptions in advance but we didn't have to pay our costs to the carrier for twelve months. Basically, we were bankrolling ourselves off the customers' money, and that's how we grew the business. As a result, we never had to take any venture capital and ended up fully owning our company and its destiny.

From the beginning, Mark always looked for ways to improve the product and find new markets. He had to improvise a lot. He says:

I've been reading a lot of stuff about iteration. We would throw something up, it wouldn't be perfect, but then we'd get so much feedback on the Web that we could quickly fix and adjust things. While we kept on modifying the product to get it to be less expensive and add more features, another vertical showed up. It was fleet-tracking business for tracking commercial service vehicles. The first customer was a tree-trimming company with twenty trucks. They said they had twenty trucks in Missouri and they needed to track them all. So we gave them twenty units and realized we were looking at a new market. . . .

We started setting up websites. We called the one for tracking small fleets of vehicles FleetLocate. Then there was a website for buying cars that we called SysLocate. A website for tracking boats was called BoatLocate. We got into this mode of *let's just try anything*. Once somebody from a different market showed interest in our service, we'd just throw up a website, modify the features, change the brand name, and put it on Google AdWords. In one week we would know whether it was the right move or the wrong one.

If there was no follow-up demand, Procon would just turn off the corresponding website. Setting up a website and features for a new vertical was a low-cost investment, because they used the same hardware and the same fulfillment process. Procon became really good at launching a whole new idea within a week. Says Mark, "It was really fun. We had a checklist of all the things that you had to do to support a new vertical."

The first units did not have an OBD-II connector, but very soon Mark's team built it in and the devices could be plugged directly into the OBD-II car port for power and odometer reading.

Soon a new market opportunity emerged that ended up propelling Mark and his company to a totally new level. Says Mark:

It almost never happens that whatever an entrepreneur sets out to do becomes the thing they end up doing. As Woody Allen once said, "Eighty percent of success is showing up." Sure enough, that's what happened to us. The original teenage driver tracking market couldn't be a big business. The cool thing that happened was that by going after the teen driver market, we found other markets. As we were marketing our tracking products, people from the other verticals were calling and e-mailing us. Our hardware and software prices were getting to the point where it made sense to put tracking devices on more and more cars, and one day we had a call from a car repossession agency.

The nature of the repossession business, as made famous by the TV show *Operation Repo*, was to recover cars sold to people with poor or no credit history who refused to or could not pay their monthly car payments, and get these cars back on the market. The repossession rate for these customers was typically 20 to 55 percent. With the ubiquity of GPS technology and affordable portable trackers, it became a no-brainer to use it to locate cars that needed to be repossessed. That, in turn, brought in financial institutions, which saw selling cars to people with no credit as an attractive business with limited risk. The market started growing rapidly, and so did Procon.

As the economy started to turn sour in 2008, more and more cars were being repossessed. This further drove demand for Procon's devices and services.

Mark's strict fiscal discipline secured not only the growth of the company, but also its independence. He says:

> I don't think we realized that we were on to something really big. There was a struggle every month. Even though I didn't want to take any venture money, I always wanted to be in a place where I *could* take venture money if I wanted it. I had to present a solid picture for the potential investors and I wasn't sure how fast I could grow. I was always doing calculations trying to figure out when my growth would

outstrip the amount of cash flow I got out of the subscriptions, because that's what was keeping the business going. If you grow too fast, you won't have enough cash coming in to pay for the inventory. I was aware of that and I was running on the ragged edge of that cycle. . . .

The other thing I learned was that every month you want to beat the month before. Well, actually, every quarter, but I told everybody at the company every month, because I figured if you get every month then you would probably get every quarter. That way, the goal for everybody in the company every month was to beat the last month's sales. It was really fun because everyone got into that and we had a ticker on everybody's computer showing how well we were doing that month. We went for twenty-five to thirty months in a row consistently beating the month before. The mentality was always: Get the sales all done before the end of the month. Some months we made it easily and some months we made it with one or two days left. We would have a brainstorming session to figure out who we could call to get more sales that month. One of my favorite memories was when one of our salespeople was running down the hall in the last minutes of the last day of the month saying, "We got the P.O., we got the month!" She was so excited.

Procon managed to sell their first two hundred thousand devices using the same design with a used cell phone, manufactured in a trailer near the beach. By the time the company grew to twenty-two employees, they had to move out of the trailer.

With unit volumes approaching hundreds of thousands, Mark had to rethink their hardware strategy. He told us:

> We hadn't envisioned selling ten thousand or twenty thousand units in a month. The problem was that once we got to a certain sales tempo, we were going to run out of phones. We couldn't buy more than ten thousand phones in a month. And we didn't want to create such demand in the market that would start jacking up the prices for used phones. We were trying to buy them without looking like we needed a lot of them. We did not want the selling auctioneers to get on to what was going on—and they never did. They thought we were just reselling them to the general market.
>
> But after about four years of four-times growth every year, we saw the writing on the wall that we'd run out of used phones. So we finally started buying tracking hardware from hardware manufacturers. By then the prices had come down quite a bit, plus, because of our volumes and installed base, we had some leverage with the hardware manufacturers. They were eager to get our business, and the prices they offered were low enough for us to start using them.

Within the next few years, Procon's volumes exceeded one million units and the company started expanding internationally. In the meantime, Procon became the largest M2M customer of T-Mobile. "We have over a million connections now with T-Mobile," says Mark. In 2011, Mark successfully sold half his company to a private equity firm.

When we asked Mark about the secrets of his success, he replied:

> Having a good idea helps, and that was kind of a good idea. But I think in the end it's two things: One is your ability to make business out of your idea without relying on too many outside entities. For example, if you need the carrier to change something so that your company can do business, ninety-nine out of a hundred entrepreneurs and companies will fail. The carrier says yes but never gets around to doing it, the entrepreneur runs out of money and the company dies. You need to have control over the way you make commerce happen, and that's why we went right to the Web. We were lucky, too, because timing is everything. Google AdWords took off and we were able to build a fleet business totally off the Internet. In fact, we built it off the Internet and got it to the next level before AdWords stopped paying as much, because everybody starting using it. . . .
>
> The second thing is just persistence and execution. It was not always easy. We had times when we put out a new product and we would find out two months later that something was failing in the field. We had to exchange hundreds, and in some cases thousands, of units in the field, work through that with the customers, doing our best to keep them happy and fix their problems. That took a lot of willpower. When those things happen it immediately costs you a lot of money. You end up with cash-flow issues. You have to do a lot of bootstrapping, be really careful

how you're managing your cash and stretching out your money and getting your customers to pay on time or early to get through. I think it's the thing all businesses face; you've got to have extreme persistence and endurance to weather through those tough times.

The success of Procon demonstrates how critical it is to build the channel and get to market fast, even before you have a perfect product. If a business can quickly iterate based on market feedback, that business will get it right eventually. We believe the same lessons apply to many areas of M2M and the Internet of Things. Often, an attempt to build just the right product results in delayed time to market, budget overages, and a lot of frustration—for the very same reasons we described at the beginning of this chapter.

Steve Hudson, chief development officer of Omnilink, launched several products in the M2M space with various partners, including the National Alzheimer's Association and the AmberWatch Foundation. He emphasizes the importance of the right channel partner. Steve says:

> For the Alzheimer's patient wearable device, we needed a channel partner that was good at merchandising, distribution, and inventory handling. At first we created relationships with partners and launched a generic product concept. Now we're at the stage where we can go back and integrate the newer technology that's more wearable and has a better form factor. I think as the category of wearable M2M devices continues to evolve, it's crucial for the new entrants to ensure proof of concept

first and then make it better and create a more end-to-end device.

Ari Silkey, CTO and co-founder of GreenLight Car, an M2M start-up, and former director of product management at Best Buy, where he used to launch a lot of connected devices, believes setting the right price for the new products in M2M is very important. It helps remove the risk in the business model for the customers. Ari also believes in the importance of retailers and distributors, because they have a lot of knowledge about price tweaking and influencing retail user behavior.

Mark Wells also believes cost is a huge factor. He says:

> In M2M it's primarily about cost. As soon as the cost of the hardware plus the service gets to the right level, all the things you thought should happen start happening. You can basically draw a price curve of where it's going and where it's been and when these M2M applications will start saving you enough money to pay for themselves. You can almost tell exactly when certain things are going to take off.

While cost is definitely a significant issue, customer awareness is just as important. Says Steve Hudson, "I think many people underestimate the amount of category awareness that's needed."

We believe educating the marketplace—bringing together the technology world and the industry—will be a very crucial step in the adoption of the Internet of Things. In this space, Peggy Smedley has been one of the pioneers. Peggy talks about marketplace education:

How do we educate the marketplace so that they know they can use M2M? You have a book; we have a magazine. We talk about it in stories, about what companies are implementing. We are completely in this digital transformation that is picking up momentum for more consumer-oriented applications. And as it continues to emerge, consumers will be continuing to adapt it. I think the more we see these applications, how they look and behave differently from one vertical market to the next—they are all created using similar kinds of fundamental building blocks, so to speak—more and more people will say, "Wow, that wirelessly connected pacemaker is designed to monitor my health and save my life." Another doctor will come with an idea that can save someone's life, using the same building blocks with even more data that can be monitored and tracked. That's how it's going to go.

Speaking about market awareness and the value for customers, Ari Silkey notes:

When you go to market with a new connected product, it's crucial to understand the end-customer experience and how they buy the product: How do they make the decision to buy the product and what are the barriers to buying the product? Not less important is how to communicate the value. Sometimes you can argue that the product can save $200, but you need a day-long seminar to explain it to your customer. That's where a lot of companies fail. Trying to make a new market is very hard, especially if you are launching a new hardware device. There's just a lot more risk with hardware.

Another critical part of getting a product to market is timing, as we have seen in the case of Procon. According to Joan Waltman, former president of Qualcomm Enterprise Services Division, "Sometimes it just takes too long for the adoption and the biggest problem [is that] you might run out of money before you make anything happen. Timing is everything."

Overall, complexity within the Machine-to-Machine ecosystem is much more significant than it was with the Internet. Non-standardized hardware, antenna design, low volumes, global connectivity, application development and design—all these elements slow down market adoption. Says John Elliott:

> We haven't seen any consistent way to connect a device to a platform and build apps across it, and run it globally or even within a region. We need a stakeholder to stand up, decide to own the ecosystem, and say they'll build an end-to-end solution, similar to what Qualcomm has done and what I see some other players are trying to do.

Considering all these challenges of getting to market, what is the best way for a company to do so today? Taking the complexity seriously is the first step. Paying attention to all aspects, starting with technology and M2M-specific aspects described in this and previous chapters, but not forgetting the user experience and distribution, will help avoid unpleasant surprises.

Another critical part is working with top talent, either internally or externally. The difference between the A and B teams is accounted for in hundreds of thousands, if not millions of dollars and many months saved or wasted in getting to market. Finally, constantly improvising, iterating, and trying different things is what will ensure that you're going to get it right eventually, as we have seen in Mark Wells' story. All that would help avoid the fate of the Kilimanjaro expedition from the Monty Python sketch: "Kilimanjaro is a pretty tricky climb, you know, most of it's up until you reach the very, very top, and then it tends to slope away rather sharply."

In the next chapter we will take a look at the investment attractiveness of the M2M space.

Chapter 7

WHERE TO INVEST

All creative people want to do the unexpected.
~ Hedy Lamarr

According to Paul Graham of Y Combinator, the best way to get start-up ideas is not to think of start-up ideas. Instead, one should focus on problems one has firsthand experience with.[29] This is great advice for both start-up and corporate entrepreneurs, but what about investors? How would investors know where to put their money if they are not familiar with the space and specific problems? Sometimes investors can take their cues from entrepreneurs, but they will also need to develop their own opinions.

Throughout this book we talked about various problems in the M2M space, from the technology ecosystem to taking

---

[29] Paul Graham, "How to Get Startup Ideas," November 2012. http://www.paulgraham.com/startupideas.html.

products to market. In this chapter we are going to spend some time zooming in on value creation and opportunities for investment. By *investment* we mean not only financial investment, but also investment of one's talent, time, and resources.

As we have seen in the previous chapters, the market opportunity for the Internet of Things is tremendous. Market forecasts are usually overly optimistic; however, the majority of experts now feel that current market forecasts are in line with market potential, and perhaps even conservative. Today, experts anticipate the market size to be larger than $700 billion by 2022, growing from about $200 billion in 2012.

Now, depending on how you segment the market and how many business fields you count in the M2M market, this number can vary greatly. The number mentioned above (by market size, starting with the largest market) includes devices, services, installation revenues, M2M platform revenues, and connectivity-related revenues. The largest industry domains today (again, by market size, starting with the largest market) are intelligent buildings, telematics, health care, and utilities.

Since investment in the Internet of Things has until now been more of a futuristic topic, and the understanding and definition of the market varies notably, forecasts are all over the place. For example, IDC, a market research firm, estimates the value of intelligent systems at $1.7 trillion already, growing to $2.4 trillion by 2017.[30]

It's interesting if you look at the high-growth markets that are currently developing around cloud computing, big data, and business intelligence. These markets are in the double-digit billions, and are often not counted toward the M2M market.

---

[30] Iain Morris, "Intelligent Systems to Drive Value in M2M Market: IDC," *Telecom Engine,* June 4, 2013. http://www.telecomengine.com/article/intelligent-systems-drive-value-m2m-market-idc.

This shows how blurry the borders are, and that we can expect a number of additional growth segments that we do not see or envision today.

The question many investors raise is: How does this growth come about? In addition, what are the core growth segments? How much of the value will be captured by existing players? How much of the market will be created by new players that either disrupt current industries or become growth leaders in the most attractive segments?

Taking a step back and looking at the big picture, one could argue that the largest potential arises from the fact that machines become more effective in doing what human beings have done in the past. As we showed in chapter 3, humans and machines work best in tandem when humans capitalize on their own creativity and intuition while machines handle data gathering, analytics, and algorithms. Already today, many systems run highly optimized with little or no human intervention, such as manufacturing, logistics planning, yield management, certain medical research, autonomous driving, and flying. Many more industry sectors will rely on machines in the future, which will take over most of the operational functions better and more precisely than humans.

The Singularity University is a nonprofit learning institution in Silicon Valley that is trying to foster knowledge and thinking in this field. According to their own proposition, they aim to "assemble, educate and inspire a cadre of leaders who strive to understand and facilitate the development of exponentially advancing technologies and apply, focus, and guide these tools to address humanity's grand challenges."[31]

---

[31] Singularity University, "What Is Singularity University?" http://singularityu.org/overview/.

While this sounds like a bold statement, many of the pieces that support this vision are coming together right now, and such programs are gaining tremendous traction.

As we mentioned in chapter 1, the key macroeconomic trends that will enable this new ecosystem to grow exponentially are described here:

First, we see reduction in size and increases in processing power, driven by Moore's Law, but also by improvements in electric power management. The second important factor is affordability—we see a strong reduction of production costs in areas like fixed and mobile networks, hardware, software, cloud computing, mobile technologies, and robotics. In most areas, technology production costs have decreased by more than 90 percent in the past several years and will continue to fall, also just as predicted by Gordon Moore and his Law. The third crucial trend is de-wireization. As more things are becoming wireless, it means their location can be almost anywhere. The growing ubiquity of cellular and Wi-Fi networks have enabled this trend. The last wire to disappear is the power cable—driven by advances in wireless power, energy harvesting, and power management.

Finally, there is another important factor, which is the network effect. This tends to show exponential growth once you have a critical mass of intelligent items and connected items that are talking to one another. The law that affects this development is Metcalfe's Law,[32] which states that the value of a network is proportional to the square of the number of con-nected users of the system. This law is applicable not only to telecommunications networks and social networks, but also to connected things, like M2M nodes. Assuming such a network

---

[32] Wikipedia, "Metcalfe's Law," http://en.wikipedia.org/wiki/Metcalfe's_law.

effect will take place, one can assume it will create huge value for the ecosystem.

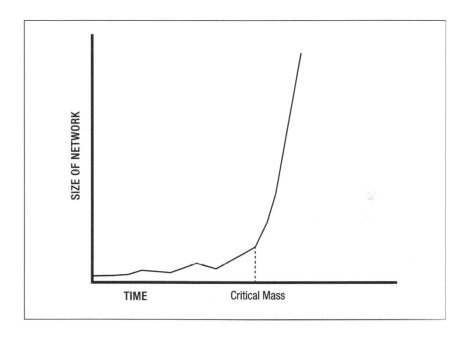

What this means for investors is that we are about to see an explosion of connected things and an explosion of data being generated. In parallel to this development, the tools and applications to generate value out of this data have become affordable to the mainstream, meaning people have access to data-analysis tools that were previously only in the hands of companies that could afford them. This perfect storm will lead to completely new applications that did not exist before.

A comparison that helps us understand the size of this new market is to see it as an extension of today's ERP systems. While the ERP core has been automated to a large extent, the periphery still consists of huge amounts of manual processes. Many of these manual inefficiencies will go away in the near future, leading to higher automation throughout the value chain into the real, physical world.

Many concepts that have been discussed in the past are becoming reality. Here are a few examples that show what is possible today.

- Imagine analyzing millions of data sets for a retailer that has implemented an RFID-based process to track millions of items. This was not possible a couple of years ago, but due to reduced costs in producing these tags, tracking them, analyzing, and giving real-time logistics, reconciliation has become possible.
- Imagine using sophisticated tracking technology to follow the flow of high-value assets around the world. Hardware, software, and connectivity costs have often made these use cases impossible to implement. Today, you can find numerous hardware manufacturers that produce reliable, robust, temperature-resistant, waterproof devices with extremely long battery life.
- Imagine storing millions of data sets of patients or athletes who are hooked to devices with a large number of sensors, which are able to track movement, exercise, and sleep behavior. In the near future we will see more and more devices that are able to track not only basic data, but also vital signs. Also, real-time blood analysis will be possible due to super-thin sensors on the skin that transmit data to the cloud, where it will be analyzed. This development, which will be much more powerful than what we see today around the *quantified self*,[33] will create a whole new health ecosystem in the near future.

---

[33] Quantified Self, "What We Are Reading," http://quantifiedself.com/.

- Imagine vending machines for drinks, snacks, or electronic devices in airports and other central locations becoming *smart* machines that will be able to track what people buy, where, and when. They will even be able to analyze who is standing in front of them and how long the buying decision takes. They will have large digital touchscreens that can run promotions at scheduled times, and they will be able to give exact data to the logistics firm to replenish products at the right time. And, of course, these machines will be connected wirelessly, and all data will be managed and stored in the cloud.

One example in the smart home/connected devices arena is about to enter the mainstream. In our opinion, one of the most successful innovations of 2012 was the Nest smart thermostat, created by Tony Fadell, who ran the teams that created the iPod and the iPhone. Tony turned beautiful design and smart functionality into significant sales in Nest's first year of commercial operations. Companies that offer home automation services, such as Control4 and Vivint (acquired in 2012 by Blackstone for $2 billion) are surging, and the decreasing cost of sensors, coupled with the growing ubiquity of smartphones, tablets, and high-speed wireless Internet, is enabling a raft of new applications.

These are just a couple of examples that show the growth potential of these markets, and the potential to create disruptive new companies and markets within a short time frame. Market opportunities for investors arise in all stages of the investment life cycle (early, late, private equity, and public markets).

In our interviews with industry experts, entrepreneurs, and visionaries, we also asked them about investment opportunities. Here is what we found out regarding markets, timing, and technology evolution.

Steve Pazol, who has a great record of building successful M2M businesses, gave some very good insights into areas of disruption and investment opportunities:

> If you're a new company and you wanted to pick a vertical, you want to look at an area that is ripe for disruption. This means that there are either a lot of assets or there are assets that are expensive to service, or perhaps there is some consumable that needs to be monitored. As long as the incumbents haven't already moved into the space, you can go in and disrupt them. Look at Square, which is a credit card processor, not really in the M2M space, but they disrupted the credit card process because they let any individual take a credit card payment. They looked at an industry that had a lot of big players and they came in and disrupted it. There are a lot of verticals with problems that can be solved with M2M.
>
> When I look into the timing question, I would evaluate what's going to cause a change in behavior. Is there a regulatory change? Is there an economic change? If you can find a macro-trend that is going to drive behavior, it makes it a lot easier. Ride that wave, rather than try to make that wave happen yourself. What you do is simplify, figure out a way that companies can do small volumes at a lower cost, or just use similar platforms, because the M2M space is the long tail of most of the economy. But if I was going to invest in Machine-to-Machine, I would probably be investing somewhere in the analytics space.

Glenn Lurie sees the largest potential in the connected home and the connected car:

> I do believe we'll see breakthroughs in automo-
> tive; I do believe we'll see breakthroughs in health
> care. I do believe we'll see some breakthroughs
> in tracking. Today we already track people, pal-
> lets, or pets with very low-cost devices. There are
> numerous opportunities with the capabilities of
> new devices that people have and what they are
> doing with them. I see two opportunities that will
> be massive as a whole: We have not yet seen a qual-
> ity, scalable platform that will be what creates the
> digital home. The second one is the automobile.
> We have not truly seen what a fully connected car
> is and can do. People are spending a good chunk
> of their life in their car and their home; those two
> places to me have the greatest opportunity as they
> get connected, get smart, and start interacting with
> you in different ways.

Mark Wells believes the vending-machine business will be a huge market in the future, and we are also noticing a lot of traction in this market. This might be due to the fact that a vending machine is already a fairly autonomous device that can run without human intervention once stocked. Adding intelligence to these machines opens the doors for a whole new way of selling products to customers in a highly auto-mated fashion.

A question we asked ourselves is: When will companies like Amazon and Walmart enter this space? Here are Mark's thoughts about this market:

I think the next one coming up that's exciting is the area of vending kiosks and digital signs. That's the next area ready to explode. One of the things that happened in the vending industry is that there's legislation that's affecting the vending-machine business. You know how you go to Starbucks and it shows the calories next to the drink? A lot of menus now have that. The legislation that got proposed in 2011 requires calorie information to be displayed on vending machines too.[34] The interesting thing is that we are at a point where it becomes realistic to use end-to-end connectivity technologies with all vending machines. The trigger point is that they need a way to display the calories on the vending machines, but they can't rely on the people to do that manually. They want to have a digital sign that displays the calories of all the different things in the machine and that is managed centrally and remotely. And it will, in turn, kick off innovations for the vending-machine business. Definitely that area is going to be the next wave, and it's a worldwide thing.

Astro Teller believes that even without massive game changers, it is possible to squeeze out huge gains from what's available now or in the near future:

We've just had this movement from disks to solid-state in the last few years that has helped on the power front, the space front, and the cost front in

---

[34] Department of Health and Human Services, "Food Labeling; Calorie Labeling of Articles of Food in Vending Machines; Proposed Rule," Federal Register, April 6, 2011. http://www.gpo.gov/fdsys/pkg/FR-2011-04-06/html/2011-8037.htm.

some cases. M2M devices also have batteries, but the energy density of batteries hasn't changed much in the past thirty years. If someone could produce something that had ten times the energy density of lithium ion, everything would change in the space. It will happen or it won't, but I think it's more productive to look at what we can do with the technologies that are already on the horizon.

An important area is how to store the energy and do the power management. At the end, whether you get the energy density up or you get the energy requirements down, it sort of doesn't matter. One can reduce energy consumption by changing the communication protocols, by changing antennas, by finding ways to be closer to each other sometimes, or to "mesh network" them in various ways. There are significant opportunities and trade-offs in the area of energy harvesting, like motion sensors, heat sensors, photovoltaic sensors, radio frequency, and so on—all offer different ways to take energy from the environment. Because once you can get there, you never need to recharge your battery. We're off by one to two orders of magnitude right now.

Another, more systematic way to look at investment opportunities is to analyze the M2M ecosystems, which we discussed in chapter 2. These ecosystems are changing as technologies evolve and mature, but, as we mentioned, here are the core areas that we see.

- Data acquisition—device hardware, which includes sensors, wireless communication devices, and so on

- Data transport—network connectivity and connectivity-related software/services
- Data analysis—software/cloud platform for data analytics/big data management
- Connected Device Platform and Application Enablement Platform—M2M software application platforms
- Installation, system integration, and professional services

With a relatively limited installed base in terms of hardware, most of the money is currently going to big data and data analytics. These areas tend to scale the fastest, and also have limited barriers to entry. Both connectivity and hardware tend to be in the hands of established players and often require significant up-front investments, so it is more difficult to enter these markets, with a few exceptions, at least for now. But especially on the hardware side, the potential for disruption is significant.

One area in the hardware space that is currently seeing significant momentum is in health and fitness devices. Companies like BodyMedia and Fitbit have shown that appealing and functional hardware, in combination with a powerful software platform that supports the leading mobile operating systems, can create significant momentum. A very important thing, as we learned earlier in this book, is to get the hardware and hardware platform right, because that is a field most of the software-focused companies continue to underestimate.

Ivo Stivoric from BodyMedia gave us some interesting clues to what is important in hardware platform design and what is important when designing health and fitness devices. He says:

> I believe if you were to look at all the APIs, you would find out that BodyMedia's are the richest and most developed. If you did an analysis of the different products, you would find that BodyMedia

has picked the part of the space that is most set up to be the hardware platform. That does not mean our device is as wearable or as fashionable as some. Jawbone has this wristband; it looks cool. The accuracy is not as good, but I think it's a nicer industrial design. Maybe it's more of a personal taste, but they have not made a bad choice in making that beautiful bracelet. In terms of accuracy, I wouldn't bet on that because there's no richness of data one can collect from the wrist. They [Jawbone] basically only have motion detection. You just cannot mine enough information from motion data alone. We figured this out twelve years ago. That's why we're doing what we're doing. The closer you get to your torso, the better data you can gather—for example, heat information, skin responses, and heart rate.[35]

Our interview with Glen Allmendinger shed some light on the two dominant players in the semiconductor space, Intel and ARM. Glen says:

For both fab and fabless[36] semiconductor companies, scale is the essence of their existence. That just means that if they can't find things in equal volume and

---

[35] Just prior to publishing, Jawbone acquired BodyMedia for over $100 million. (Source: Lauren Goode, "Jawbone Acquires BodyMedia for More Than $100 Million, as Wearable Tech Gets More Intense," *All Things D.* http://allthingsd.com/20130430/jawbone-acquires-bodymedia-for-more-than-100-million-as-wearable-tech-gets-more-intense/.)

[36] Fabless manufacturing is the design and sale of hardware devices and semiconductor chips, while outsourcing the fabrication, or "fab" of the devices to a specialized manufacturer called a semiconductor foundry. (Source: http://en.wikipedia.org/wiki/Fabless_manufacturing.)

at equal margin, they're dead. In fact, if you look at things like stuffing silicon in the meters and you want to be able to support that device for ten-plus years, a company like Intel may have more control over the life cycle of these devices than anybody else because they own the fabs. If you flip to the ARM side of the world, they've got a fantastic position potentially, but even the ARM-based chipset OEMs often neglect the Internet of Things because it does not seem to offer scale right away. In many respects, that's just an ecosystem-wide view of what goes on.

We believe there are multiple investment opportunities in hardware—despite the traditional reluctance of investors to enter this space. In the Internet of Things, opportunities in hardware spread from new energy- and cost-optimized silicon to vertically integrated devices for specific markets. There are tremendous opportunities in figuring out the whole data-acquisition space—sensor calibration and integration; hardware platforms, which would allow building of new devices as quickly and cheaply as mobile phones today; smart and self-tuning antennas, which would fit small enclosures without losing signal strength; energy management and harvesting, which includes various sensors, capacitors, and new types of flexible or even spray-on batteries; and many more.

For example, Glen Allmendinger observes:

I would say there's still a lot that can be done in device management. This is another example of where everybody's trying to take the pre-existing set of pieces and bend them to do the correct things. There's probably great room for innovation in that realm. If you think about what's required to manage a device, I need to know where it is, I need to know if it's on or off, I need to know maybe some other significant variables about its operation, and I need to know all of that in real time.

Also, as we mentioned in earlier chapters, there are still no players who provide M2M hardware end-to-end. Many start-up and midsize companies end up developing their own hardware, because there is nobody they can go to. Ideally, they would much rather focus on the software or services and rely on somebody else to provide hardware. We heard this theme from several market experts, but specifically from Astro Teller and Steve Hudson, who both emphasized this point.

We believe an opportunity for a virtual OEM specifically in the M2M space is ripe. The market is ready for a player who would dramatically shorten the hardware development time and optimize the time to market for its customers. As long as this player figures out how to churn hardware versions faster and at a low cost—just as we are seeing today with smartphones—it will enable much more rapid innovation to happen in this space.

We feel like the hardware space in M2M somewhat resembles the computer space before the emergence of the PC (or Apple II for that matter). There are multiple form factors with different requirements, different use cases, and different software. However, once a common denominator–type of device emerges, it will take the market by storm.

In data transport or connectivity, most of the market is dominated by telecom carriers. They have invested tremendous assets into mobile networks with high coverage in urban and regional areas. They also have developed significant footprints for global roaming capabilities. This is what made the cellular networks pretty much ubiquitous. An area that saw some momentum in this space was connectivity management. Here, companies like

Jasper Wireless have established traction by partnering with operators and building a global footprint through their M2M connectivity management platform. There is also an opportunity for M2M-focused Mobile Virtual Network Operators (MVNOs), who would not be burdened by the legacy voice business and can just approach the Internet of Things space with services in mind. We heard this point expressed by Ioannis Fikouras. Aside from that, innovation in this space is limited.

The M2M software application platform space has not seen a player gaining mass-market adoption. Here, Google's Android is the most often-used platform; however, this is still a highly fragmented market with a number of niche players, but, more importantly, with a huge amount of customization and professional services involved. What people tend to confuse is that apps for M2M have very different requirements than most consumer-focused apps we see today. The complexity, and therefore future opportunities, will mostly be found in the systems application layer, which connects the complex dots. Glen Allmendinger gives some very profound advice:

> Probably much larger in my mind is the applications foray. What people don't realize about app development in this space is that all of the device management–related data has almost equal value to the primary data that device sends. Device management by itself takes you almost 50 percent toward being able to create new applications.

> The way we've organized our thinking is that to avoid terms like *middleware* that everyone hears and says and thinks about differently, we just say there's a system application layer. There's a whole bunch of state-based routines, monitoring routines,

diagnostic routines, ID, and securing routines. The
important opportunity is that if you understand how
the data is configured from those kinds of routines,
it creates application value by itself. In other words,
it's the intersection of unstructured, structured, and
time-based data. Nobody really knows today how
to turn that into an application. But that's a rich
ground for making a lot of money in the future. If
I were looking medium to longer term, the whole
data-brokerage story and information architecture
would be the place I would look.

Installations and professional services are a huge segment
today, and will continue to be a large segment in the future, even
though service revenues are expected to decline when markets
mature. The core of revenues will most likely be generated by
large system integrators like IBM and Accenture; however, we
can expect to see a couple of new services players in high-growth
markets that are more agile and flexible to ride that wave.

We also expect to see a number of players that offer a compelling product in combination with service offerings, like in
big data, where we saw a number of aggressive new market
entrants that provided big data as a service, a combination
of hardware/software solutions and consulting/professional
services and training.

International markets can offer attractive growth opportunities. Depending on how fast and frictionless a product or
service can scale globally, and how strong existing assets of a
company can be leveraged, there will be a huge market to tackle.
Regulatory restrictions will also lead to business opportunities
in other countries, where regulation is less strict. Specifically
in health care, one can assume there will be significant innovation coming from less-regulated markets. This innovation,

once proven, will then be deployed in markets like the United States or Europe.

The growth of innovative companies in all these fields will lead to mergers and acquisitions activities of large players. Many of them will wake up to the fact that there are a number of pieces missing in their solutions portfolio. You will find smaller players who have figured out bits and pieces because the larger players have been too slow, and the large players will start buying those small pieces. This becomes an appealing environment for early-stage investors in this field.

Overall, the investment opportunities can be divided between the vertical—serving a specific industry or a specific use case—and the horizontal—serving the whole ecosystem. In the first case, it's easier to define problems and build solutions that would work well within a particular vertical. Often, systems built in the process of delivering a vertical solution can be applied to other verticals. The systems that have achieved proven success in more than one vertical will become horizontal in time. One example is the SysDevX platform developed by Procon.

On the other side, there are many horizontal ecosystem data-flow issues that are ripe for resolution. Specifically, on the data mining and statistical analysis of data as well as on the data acquisition side—hardware—that's where we believe the most opportunities for innovation and investment are.

But at the end of the day, the best investment opportunities are going to be driven by very well-defined problems that the Internet of Things will help solve: increased visibility, increased productivity, reduced guesswork, better risk management, and better connection to our environment.

CONCLUSION

You have just finished reading *The Silent Intelligence: The Internet of Things*, a book that took us more than a year and a half to write. Quite a few things have changed in that time because the space has been growing so fast. Some of the things we viewed as hypotheses at the beginning became proven, companies merged, new entrants came in, and there have also been several successful exits for investors in this space.

All these events point to the rapid growth of the Internet of Things, as more opportunities emerge and more companies jump on the M2M bandwagon. M2M is impossible to deny or ignore—it's here to stay, and it will change our lives and the ways we do business in more profound ways than we can even imagine today. The impact of the Internet of Things will be comparable to that of the Web in the '90s, but some think it will be more like the impact of the Industrial Revolution.

"So far, everything on the Internet, with a few exceptions, is produced by humans. We are moving to the world where most of the Internet content and traffic will be produced by things," said Kevin Ashton. We can only imagine how much this development will change the world around us.

For many companies, venture capitalists, and other investors, it's important not to wait too long, but to embrace the world of the Internet of Things and get involved in projects, because this is the only way to learn about the space. Of course, it is important to build the initial understanding of the space, its challenges, and its opportunities, and that's why we wrote this book.

Companies that are waiting for the market to arrive and start buying gizmos in large quantities—this moment may never come. If you're waiting for the moment when customers in the M2M space will start buying millions of your chips or devices or connections or sensors, this may or may not happen. Instead, the market might choose a different chip or a different sensor from a market player you don't even know exists. Don't wait for that to happen. The time is now to start understanding the market and its trends, tweak your gizmo so that it fits the new market requirements, keep tweaking it until it fits, and make sure it fits within the entire ecosystem. This ecosystem may be very different from the one you are used to, but working with real customers will open your eyes to who your new partners and suppliers may be.

This brings us to another point: the current disconnect between the high-tech community and the industry in the M2M space. It appears that in most conferences and industry events it's the techies who are talking among themselves and complaining that the M2M market is not happening soon enough.

It is already happening, and the best way to embrace it is to work closely with the industry—with the consumers of M2M technology, with banks, insurance companies, industrial companies, utilities, automotive companies, municipalities, and so on. Once the bridges are built with the industry, once the tech community starts understanding in much more detail what the real problems in the industry are that can be solved with M2M, a lot of new and exciting things will happen. It will unleash new opportunities, applications, and business models, which will further drive the adoption of the Internet of Things.

Building communities around the Internet of Things will also help advance consumer awareness and open up new possibilities.

With *The Silent Intelligence* as a starting point, we plan to contribute, and we view this book as the beginning of a journey. Many excerpts from the interviews we conducted for this book did not make it into this book because of the format or context; however, we plan to publish them on our blog, along with new interviews and other notable publications. We look forward to continuing the dialogue with our readers on our website, thesilentintelligence.com.

Yours,

Daniel Kellmereit and Daniel Obodovski

San Francisco, July 2013

ACKNOWLEDGMENTS

This book would have never seen the light of day were it not for the many people who helped us on our journey.

First of all, we would like to thank all the people we interviewed and whose contributions are essential and invaluable for the success of this book. We'd like to thank Glen Allmendinger of Harbor Research, Kevin Ashton of Belkin, Assaf Biderman of MIT's SENSEable City Lab, Christian Busch of SAP, Bill Davidson of Qualcomm, John Elliott of Accenture, Ioannis Fikouras of Ericsson, Steve Hudson of Omnilink, Dr. Peter Kuhn of Scripps Research Institute, Glenn Lurie of AT&T, John Major of MTSG, Panos Nasiopoulos of the University of British Columbia, Dermot O'Shea of Taoglas, Steve Pazol of Qualcomm, Dr. Sanjay Sarma of MIT, Ari Silkey of BestBuy and Zubie, Peggy Smedley of *Connected World*, Ivo Stivoric of Body Media, Astro Teller of Google, Bill Toone of ECOLIFE Foundation, Joan Waltman, former Sr. Vice President and Division President at Qualcomm Enterprise Services, and Mark Wells of Procon. In addition to these people, we had innumerable encounters with professionals in the M2M/IOT space who encouraged us and gave us interesting insights for this book.

With much gratitude, we want to thank Steve Pazol, our mentor for *The Silent Intelligence*, who provided great advice and insights into topics, writing, and promotion. He was also kind enough to write the foreword to this book.

We would also like to thank our colleagues and managers who believed in us and supported this undertaking at our respective companies. Specifically, Daniel Kellmereit would like to thank Francis Deprez, CEO of Detecon International and Daniel Obodovski would like to thank Ahmad Jalali, VP of Engineering at Qualcomm.

Matt Oesterle was extremely helpful in explaining to us all the steps in the self-publishing process and introducing us to the key people. Our editor, Shanna Trenholm, spent many days and weeks questioning our original sentences and making the book text (and our website copy) more enjoyable to read; Sophia Daly provided graphic design for our webpage and for all social media sites. Beth Adelman did the final copyediting and source checking. We also want to thank Chris Szwedo for creating our amazing promotional video.

In preparation, we used the services of the rev.com (formerly foxtranscribe.com) for transcribing all the interviews in a fast and cost-efficient manner; we also used 99design.com for the graphic design of the book cover. The interior template design, eBook layout and the final proofreading were provided by 1106 Design.

Finally, we would like to thank our respective families for supporting us throughout this journey.

Made in the USA
San Bernardino, CA
19 December 2013